Secrets of Tracing

Your Ancestors

Whether you're a beginner or have already delved into do-it-yourself genealogy, this up-to-date, concise, informa- tion-packed book will show you everything you need to know about tracing your ancestors! Quillen reveals the secrets the pros use in a logical, step-by-step approach in a way that's fun and easy to follow. If you apply the advice in "Secrets of Tracing Your Ancestors," you'll learn all the essential tools needed to begin your quest of discovery into your family background – and you'll learn something about yourself as well!

About the Author

For the past twenty years, W. Daniel Quillen has been a professional writer specializing in travel and technical subjects. He has taught beginning genealogy courses to university students and working adults, and is a frequent lecturer in beginning and intermediate genealogy classes in Colorado. He has compiled his years of genealogical training and research into *Secrets of Tracing Your Ancestors*. He lives in Centennial, Colorado with his wife and six children. If you would like to contact him about anything in this book, his e-mail address is: danielmcq@juno.com.

Secrets of Tracing
Your Ancestors

W. Daniel Quillen

Cold Spring Press

Cold Spring Press

P.O. Box 284, Cold Spring Harbor, NY 11724
E-mail: Jopenroad@aol.com

ISBN 1-892975-88-2
Library of Congress Control Number: 2002117524

Notice: FamilySearch is a registered trademark of Intellectual Reserve, Inc.

This book is dedicated to my grandparents, as well as to all those whose life's passion is discovering their roots.

Table of Contents

13. Ethnic Research   119

14. Is Anyone Out There?   140

15. Professional Genealogists   144

Sidebars, Charts & Logs

Remember me in the family tree –
My name, my days, my strife;
Then I'll ride upon the wings of time
And live an endless life.

1. Introduction

It's like going home to a place you've never been before, or like meeting family for the first time and having a feeling you've always known them.

Genealogy. Family History. Tracing your Ancestors. By any name it is one of the most exciting, challenging, fun, insightful, delicious and intriguing things you will ever do. It can become more than a hobby – it can become a passion and an obsession (but the good kind!).

Not only is genealogy considered the number 1 hobby in America, some experts believe it is the number 1 hobby in the world. But why? Why has this seemingly sedentary hobby overtaken the scintillating pastime known as philatelia (stamp collecting)?

Perhaps it is in our very DNA. In the Judeo-Christian tradtion, our first parents (Adam and Eve) kept a genealogy, as did their descendants: the Bible is rife with genealogies from the Old Testament to the New Testament (remember all those "begats?"). In this vein, family bibles often contain rich genealogical information for those individuals lucky enough to have them in their possession.

During America's bicentennial year, Alex Haley wrote and published a book called *Roots*. It was a history of his family from southern slavery to his ancestor's early life in a remote West African village. The ABC network made it into an epic twelve-hour mini-series. About 1.6 million Americans tuned in, and over the eight days that *Roots* was on TV, the genealogical flame in America flared high. As a result of Alex Haley's search for his ancestors, many of us were inspired to search out our own roots. Today, that genealogical flame continues to burn in the hearts and souls of many Americans.

Genealogy is a hobby that can consume you. You'll find it as addictive as eating potato chips and as satisfying as watching a lovely sunset at the end of a hard day's work. There will be times when you will spend many hours, then other times when you put it down for a bit. But like a good friend (or family member!), you can easily pick up where you left off.

Through the pages of this guide, I'll show you the professional genealogist's secrets. You'll learn how to begin researching your ancestors. I'll tell you the errors I made in doing research so that you can avoid them. I have provided easy-to-follow instructions and no-nonsense counsel on how to begin, proceed and succeed in this great endeavor. I'll introduce you to more than a few common genealogical hurdles, along with suggestions on how to overcome them.

The Internet has touched almost all areas of our society, and it has proven to be a huge boon to genealogists. As you read, you'll learn how to get the most out of the Internet for researching your family history.

Throughout the book I show samples of forms that may be of use to you. If you e-mail me at the address listed in the front of this book, I will be happy to e-mail you any of the forms you find in the book. I'll even be happy to provide any guidance I can if you run into problems in your research.

I have also provided in-depth advice on researching various ethnic origins, including African-American, Jewish, Irish, Hispanic and Native American roots, as well as general information on succeeding in research for those ethnic groups not covered in-depth here.

So come along and follow me as we meander our way through old censuses, pore over church records, and find new and exciting ways to discover and learn more about your ancestors. I promise it will be a trip you're glad you took!

2. Why Genealogy?

Why is genealogy so popular?

Many societies – Asian, Native American, African and others – kept accurate and extensive genealogies that extended back for hundreds, even thousands of years. Many of them were kept in the memories of tribal Elders and passed on in the oral tradition, spiced with stories of heroism and tragedy from the lives of their forbears.

One might even argue (successfully, I think), that the dusty hobby/ livelihood of archaeology is nothing more than an effort to find man's earliest roots – in other words — genealogy!

Nearly since the birth of the United States, Americans have been interested in who they were and where they came from. Scarcely a dozen years after the signing of the Declaration of Independence, the first census of the United States was commissioned by Congress, and censuses have continued unabated every decade since that time. Our Founding Fathers

GENEALOGICAL HUMOR?

Years ago I was in Richmond, Virginia on business. Since many generations of my family lived and died in Virginia, I decided to stay a few extra days after my business trip to sift through the many genealogical records that can be found in the Virginia State Library there. I mentioned to my work associate that I was going to stay in Richmond a few days after my business was completed.

She said, "Oh, do you have family here?"

I replied, "Yes, but they are all dead."

Dead silence followed. My explanation about staying to do some genealogical research seemed to calm her consternation (a bit).

weren't merely interested in counting the people. The earliest US censuses counted families. They listed the names of heads of households, as well as the age ranges of members of the family and their sex. Since that time, the census instrument has been refined to provide us with great detail on the lives of our progenitors – names, age, sex, number of children, occupation, home owner or renter, and the state or country of the individual's parents' birth.

Before you set out on your genealogical journey, let's set one thing straight. The hobby you are involved in is spelled GeneAlogy, not GeneOlogy. That third syllable, however, can be pronounced either like *al* or *awl* – it makes no difference. By if you are going to pick up genealogy as a hobby, let's make sure you spell it correctly!

Before we go much further, let me introduce you to my family. As we go through the book, you'll get to know us better, as I will use many of us to illustrate various aspects and methods of genealogical research.

I am William Daniel Quillen, and I am married to the lovely Bonita Blau Quillen. We have six children. My parents are William Edgar Quillen and Versie Lee Lowrance. They had three children.

My grandparents were:
• Helon Edgar Quillen and Vivian Iris Cunningham. They had one child.
• Elzie Lee Lowrance and Alma Hudson. They had three children.

My great grandparents were:
• Edgar Estil Quillen and Theodora Charity McCollough
• William Edward Cunningham and Emma Adelia Sellers
• Thomas Newton Lowrance and Margaret Ellen Turpin
• Francis Marion Hudson and Margaret Ann McClure

My 2nd great grandparents were:
• Jonathan Baldwin Quillen and Sarah Minerva Burke
• William Lindsay McCollough and Lucy Arabella Phillips
• William Huston Cunningham and Amanda Stunkard
• John Thomas Sellers and Celeste Elizabeth Horney
• Jeremiah Hudson and Frances Duvall

My 3rd great grandparents were:
• Charles Franklin Quillen and Susan or Susannah _____
• Samuel McCollough and Elizabeth Throckmorton
• Oliver Sayers Phillips and Charity Graham
• Joseph Cunningham and Sarah Rogers
• Matthew Stunkard and Margaret Peoples
• John T. Sellers and Elizabeth Ritchey
• Leonidas Horney and Jane Crawford

As we progress through the book, I'll use some of these individuals to illustrate search techniques, discrepancy resolution, and perhaps most basically, a much better way to list this information!

GENEALOGY AT WORK

There are many advantages to doing genealogy that go beyond collecting the names of ancestors and putting them in a notebook on your shelf. Here are a few I have come up with, but this is by no means an exhaustive list. You can use the information to:

- come up with meaningful (and sometimes different) names for your children;
- determine a health genealogy (do you have a history of specific ailments in your family that you may want to guard against: heart disease, diabetes, alcoholism, cancer, etc?);
- establish membership in patriotic organizations like The Daughters of the American Revolution;
- meet new friends. Genealogists are among the friendliest people you'll ever meet;
- justify an international vacation (research trip!) to the land of your ancestors' nativity;
- get out of the house: prowling through cemeteries, old courthouses and other places of immense interest.

3. Get Started

As they say, the longest journey begins at home, and your genealogical adventure need not begin anywhere but within your own home. Start with yourself. A key element of genealogy is to provide information about yourself for your posterity. Now, you may not think that you lead a very exciting life, or that no one would ever be interested in learning about you and your life. But before you know it, you'll have children and grandchildren, even great grandchildren, who would be extremely interested in your life.

Gather all the information about your life that you can find. As you begin thinking and looking, you'll be surprised by the amount of information that is available about you. Here are a few to consider:

Birth Certificates

Birth certificates provide a wealth of information, and are considered a primary source in genealogical research. Consider the information that is generally provided on a birth certificate:

• Your birth date and place;
• full names of your father and mother;
• your parents' address;
• often, your parents' birthplaces;
• occasionally, your parents' occupations.

Remember – just because you know all of this doesn't necessarily mean that a grandson who is interested in learning about you 60 years from now will know it too. His father (your son) may remember some details, but a birth certificate will provide a wealth of information – all accurate. It may also provide the thread to further research, as it provides important information about your parents and their birthplaces. The first time you find a birth certificate of a long-deceased relative you'll know what I mean.

It is not necessary to go to a lot of expense to do this – a photocopy will be fine for your genealogical purposes. There is no need to go to the additional time and expense to get a certified copy, unless you want to.

Baptismal or Confirmation Certificates

Church records such as these often contain as much information about you and your parents as a birth certificate does. In addition, it gives your descendants an idea of your religious convictions – or at least those of your parents.

Graduation Diplomas

While not generally a wealth of genealogical information, high school and college graduation diplomas may shed a little light on your education as well as where you lived as a teen and young adult. These kinds of threads, if found for your ancestors during your genealogical research, might lead you to find the spouse of that ancestor, or perhaps even a sibling or two, especially if the reason you went to that educational institution was because your family moved near there.

Newspaper Articles

Does your local newspaper have a column listing recent births? If so, did your mother clip it out of the newspaper when you were born? It will likely include your parents' names and their address. Were you a superb athlete that was mentioned frequently on the sports pages? As interesting as those articles are to you, you can bet they will be for your grandchildren. How about obituaries? I don't suppose you'll cut your own obituary out, but what about those for your parents, grandparents, etc? Obituaries can be very brief, or they can be very detailed and provide extensive genealogical information about this ancestor of yours. On more than one occasion I have found an obituary that provided a piece of the family history puzzle I was working on for a particular ancestor, and that puzzle piece clarified the picture sufficiently for me to find other puzzle pieces.

Were you involved in plays? Did a newspaper article feature your one-man/one-woman art show at the local library? Did you win a local piano competition? Or did your prize steer win Best-in-Class at the local 4-H competition? All of these would be of interest to your descendants.

Was there an article in the local newspaper when you went into the service, or when you became engaged? These too would be good to include in your genealogical collection about you.

Photographs

All right — confess. You have hundreds, perhaps thousands of family pictures – and not a single one is in a labeled photo album, nor do any of them have a single thing written on the backs of them, much less basic information such as who is pictured and the date of the picture. Don't dismay – you are not alone. This can be a huge project in and of itself. In fact, an entire industry has sprung up around photo albums.

However, it isn't necessary to get real fancy or painstakingly detailed, nor is it necessary to spend hundreds of hours cataloging and mounting photos. I'm suggesting just the basics here. You don't need to write on every picture in all those boxes and closets – just go through that mammoth pile and begin gleaning photos from various stages of your life – infancy, childhood, adolescence, young adulthood, early marriage, etc. If you have just one or two photos (or three or four) from each period of your life that would be a wonderful start. Write on the backs of these photos as much information as you can remember. If you can't remember what year a photo was taken, just approximate: "Dad and me at Lake Isabel in southern Colorado when I was 12 or 13 – about 1968 or 1969." Some information will be far better than none.

PRECIOUS HISTORY DISCOVERED

In my role as family genealogist, I pestered my grandmother for years for information about her family. She shared a few small photos of her parents when they were in their 80s. After my grandmother's death, my parents went to Oklahoma to help my grandfather pack up the house so that he could move in with them in their home in Colorado.

While going through their personal effects of nearly 60 years of marriage, my parents discovered a box in the corner of their old Model T garage that contained perhaps 400 photographs in it. Each picture had been meticulously labeled by my great grandmother with the date the photo was taken and the names of all individuals in the photo.

The photos were of several lines of our family, and I was able to match the information on the photos with the genealogy this great grandmother had written in the center section of the family Bible.

It was a remarkable find, a precious discovery.

Government Documents

Sometimes we have experiences in our lives that go on permanent file with the government, and for a small fee you can get copies of documents. Included here are military papers and marriage or divorce records.

Memorabilia

Did you keep the tickets from the Dodgers game your dad took you to when you were 6 years old when you were on vacation in Los Angeles? How about those tickets to the Broadway play *The King and I* when you and your sweetheart were first married? While they may have faded with age, you can be assured they will be of great interest to your descendants some day. So gather all that information out of the shoe boxes on the top shelf of your closet, or the top right-hand drawer of your dresser, etc.

Some documents that fall into the Memorabilia category are those associated with your family: the program from a funeral for a grandparent, the program from your child's baptism and so on. Be sure to include these in your collection as they will provide information about you and those you loved to those who follow.

Miscellaneous

This list isn't exhaustive – I have just provided a few of the more obvious items with which to begin your genealogical collection. If you run across other items during your genealogical foraging that you think will be of interest to your posterity, by all means keep it.

Now that you have gathered all this information for yourself, expand the search to each and every member of your household. Do it for your spouse and children – no one in your current household should be immune from your quest!

Shifting Gears

Up to this point, you have been gathering what I call physical genealogical evidence – birth certificates, diplomas, church and government records, etc. Now it is time to shift gears and begin gathering genealogical *information* – the intangible information that you need to help you identify your ancestors. And the best place to start? With yourself.

Yes – that's right – begin with yourself again. You may be surprised by how much you already know, especially about those relatives that are closest to you – your siblings, parents and grandparents. Start with each person, and write down everything you know: full name, nicknames, date of birth, birthplace, places lived, etc. Unless you are absolutely certain, I would check the information with each person after you have written it down. A personal visit, phone call, e-mail or letter are all appropriate, depending on your individual circumstances.

Once you have captured everything you know, it is time to work with members of your extended family to find out what knowledge they have about the family. This is a valuable way to spend your time, especially since many of these family members may be aging and once they leave this earthly existence their knowledge will go with them.

Most genealogy guides suggest beginning with your parents. I suppose I will support that suggestion, although I will do so with one *caveat*. Almost every family I know of has someone – generally an older relative – who is considered the family genealogist, or if not the family genealogist, the one person in the family who just seems have an interest in and who remembers all the pertinent facts about the family. In my case, it is my Great Aunt Ruth, my grandfather's sister. Of all my extended relatives, she seems to be the one who has the most interest in and knowledge of the history of the family.

If you have an "Aunt Ruth" in your family, then I would suggest starting with her. If she lives in town or nearby, then arrange to meet her to talk about the family. If it is not practical because of distances, then the telephone is a wonderful genealogical instrument. E-mail is a possibility, but I find most of the people from my grandfather's generation are not computer literate. Finally, the postal service is another possibility.

Okay, so you have settled on your family's Aunt Ruth to begin with. What do you do? Where do you begin? Well, first, you need a plan. What are you going to ask? What information is most necessary for you to find out, and what information is she likely to be able to supply? Here are some questions you might consider asking her:

- What was your father's full name? Did he use any nicknames?
- Where was he born?
- When was he born (at least the year)?
- Did he ever leave his hometown? If so, where did he go, and why?
- What did he do for a living?
- Was he ever in the military?
- What were his parents' names? Where were they from? Do you remember his mother's maiden name?
- Did he have any siblings? How many? Was he the oldest, youngest, in the middle?
- Do you know the names of his siblings? How about their ages? (Was Aunt Susie two years younger than your dad?)
- What did he look like? Do you have any pictures of him? Who would have some if you don't?

And don't forget these kinds of questions:

- What are your favorite recollections of him?
- Did he have a sense of humor? Or a hot temper (that runs in my family!)?
- Did he love animals?
- What did he do for fun and relaxation?
- What do you miss most about him?
- What are some of your favorite stories from his life?

After you finish getting information about her father (your great grand-father), ask those same questions about her mother, her brothers and sisters, her aunts and uncles, etc. It may not be possible to get all the genealogical information you would like in one visit, so plan to come again.

As you glean information from older relatives, be sure and try to get more than just facts and figures. See if they remember any stories about their parents or grandparents that they can share. Did great grandpa have some hair-raising war stories? Any close calls faced by family members through the years? Ask questions about their health - especially what their cause of death was. Information like this may provide you with important health information for yourself. You'll learn whether there is a history of diabetes / heart disease / stroke, etc., that might be very good for you to know. If several generations of the men in your family died of heart attacks in their 50s, it would be a good thing for you to know and attend to.

When interviewing, pretend you are in school. Date your paper. Put your name on it. Write down who you are interviewing. You may think you'll always remember those things, but after a few years the specifics will fade, I guarantee you.

My editor once gave me the key to being a successful travel guide writer, and I think it applies to genealogists too, especially as it relates to interviewing relatives. He said, "You must be curious. Don't just get the facts, get the facts behind the facts." So - be curious.

Be sure and ask for maiden names, nicknames and pet names. My great grandmother was named Theodora Charity McCollough, but everyone called her Dolly. And her mother was always called Grandma Mac.

Caution!

One caution here – don't make this feel like an inquisition. Make it a pleasant experience. If your Aunt Ruth is comfortable with it, bring a video camera and set it off to the side (so she can hopefully forget it is even there), and just let her talk. If a video camera isn't a possibility, then try a tape recorder. Again, if she is more comfortable try keeping it out of sight so as not to intimidate her. Ideally, you can glean the information by just having her talk about her daddy. Occasionally you might supply a question or two (from the list above or others that occur to you throughout the course of the conversa-tion) that will redirect the conversation. But don't be in a rush to get the information and get out the door – this has the potential of being a great time for both of you. You get to learn first-hand information about one of your ancestors, and your Aunt Ruth gets to reminisce about her dad – a win-win situation for all parties concerned.

During the course of your visit, determine whether she has any documents that might further your quest for information. Often, as one of the few in the family who are interested, birth certificates, death certificates, marriage certificates, etc., find their way to the Aunt Ruth in each family. Ask to see them, and come prepared to copy information from them. If there is time and an opportunity, you may wish to see if she will allow you to photocopy the documents.

A 35mm camera is good for taking photographs of photographs that your Aunt Ruth may have. I have several photos of ancestors that look nearly as good as the originals themselves. For best results, use muted natural light. This can be accomplished on a day that is slightly overcast, or under a shaded patio during a sunny day. You can use the same camera for taking pictures of various documents if a photocopier isn't available.

Another word of caution here: Be careful – don't take as Gospel the memories of your relatives, even the Aunt Ruth of your family. Sometimes you can end up on a wild goose chase. For example, one relative thought my great grandmother was born in Arkansas. I spent a great deal of time searching Arkansas for her and her family with no luck. Then, when I mentioned my dead-ends to another relative, she responded with, "Well, that's because she wasn't born in Arkansas - she was born in Texas. She was embarrassed that she was born there, so she told everyone she was born in Arkansas." So – recognize this information for what it often is: the best knowledge available at the time. It can lead you to real treasures, or it can lead you down the wrong paths.

Finally, be persistent. I had been searching for the birth information for a great aunt of mine. Family tradition held that she was born in Cottonwood, Kansas. A search of vital records there turned up her three brothers, but not her. One time when I was fresh off another disappointing dead end on this great aunt, I was visiting my folks while on a business trip. While I was there, my grandfather's three sisters and a cousin dropped in for a visit. I once again asked my Aunt Ruth about Aunt Agnes, and she once again confirmed her understanding that Agnes was born in Cottonwood Falls, Kansas. At that point, the cousin (who I had never before met, nor have I seen since) piped in and said that No, Agnes hadn't been born in Cottonwood Falls, and that the family moved there when she was a little girl. She thought they had lived in Sharon Springs before moving to Cottonwood Falls. A search of the county birth records for Sharon Springs confirmed it as my Aunt Agnes' birthplace.

For the record, these kinds of coincidences *happen all the time* for genealogists. When my great aunts and their cousin dropped by for a visit with my folks, I just happened to have been there from my home in New Jersey and my aunts had driven up from Oklahoma to my parents' Denver home.

Other Records
When you are visiting older relatives (including your parents!), they often have information-oozing genealogical records around their house in old

trunks, in attics or in the rafters of the old garage. Here are a few items that often provide genealogical information:

Old Letters

If you can lay your hands on old family letters, they can shed a great deal of light on your family. They provide a peek into their lives. And they often contain information about the family that either confirms information you already have, or that sends you off on a search to confirm information contained therein. A letter written by your great grandmother to her "Dearest Sister Sadie," can be a great clue, especially if you never knew that she had a sister named Sadie!

Years ago I found a letter my great grandmother wrote to her brother. She had spent time with their sister during the last week of that sister's life. The sister was dying of diabetes-related health problems, and my great grandmother was briefing her brother on many aspects of the family. From the letter, I learned:

• her sister's name
• her brother's name
• her sister's husband's name
• the names of all of her sister's children
• the date of her sister's death
• the place of her sister's death
• that her sister's parents lived in the same town where she lived.

In addition to these important facts, I got a peek into my great grandmother's heart and soul. I felt the pain she must have felt as she described her sister's suffering. I felt the great love she had for this sister and for her sister's family.

Do you have any old family letters? Do any of your older relatives? It may surprise you to learn that there are indeed these kinds of pages of your family's history in existence in old trunks, attics, boxes in the rafters of old garages, etc. Remember, several generations ago letters were the only contact family members often had with one another, and letters were filed away as treasures to be visited many times.

Old Budgets/Ledgers

One of my favorite genealogical finds was a budget my mother wrote down when she and my father were first married. It provided a fascinating peek into their lives at that time, and was probably a fair representation of the American working class at that time in our nation's history. Entries included such things as rent ($55), groceries ($10), utility bills ($12), gas ($10). Of course, this was at a time when my father made $48 per week as a telephone lineman.

Is there something similar in your family? Entries might include information about an ancestor's business or investing decisions. It might include loans to children, siblings or parents (or from any of those sources).

GENEALOGY TERMS

Since you are going to be learning about genealogy, it only makes sense for you to learn the language. Following are some terms that you will want to know and understand (for a more complete glossary, see Appendix A):

Family Group Sheet – this is a document that groups a family together under their father. Included will be a man, his wife and all of his children, along with important information about each person, such as their birth, marriage and death dates and places. It is one of the main forms used in genealogy research.

Family History Center – genealogy libraries staffed by volunteers of the LDS Church where genealogists can access the LDS Church's vast genealogical records. They are open to any genealogist, regardless of religious persuasion.

GED.COM – a standard software format that most genealogy software uses as a standard. If you are using a genealogy program that uses GED.COM, you will be able to share your information with others more easily.

Maternal – used to describe which line of the family tree you are referring to. Your maternal grandfather is your mother's father.

Paternal – used to describe which line of the family tree you are referring to. Your paternal grandfather is your father's father.

Pedigree Chart – this is a chart the will show at a glance what your "family tree" looks like, by showing in graphic form who your parents, grandparents, great grandparents, etc., are. A limited amount of genealogical information is included. This too is an important genealogical form.

Primary Source – these are genealogy records created at the time of the event. A birth certificate would be considered an original record.

Secondary Source – genealogy records where information is provided much later than the event. A tombstone or death certificate would be considered a primary source for death information, but a secondary source for birth information, since it is likely that the birth information was provided many years after the person's birth occurred.

Vital Records – this is the term used to refer to an individual's birth, marriage and death.

Family Bibles

Well, if your family kept an old family Bible, you are lucky indeed. My great grandmother completed numerous generations of genealogy in the center section of her old family Bible, and it is one of my most precious possessions.

But let me provide this warning about the information you find in family Bibles - it should be considered a secondary source. Unless you know for sure that all the names, dates and places contained in the Bible were written at the time they occurred, you must consider them as secondary sources. Good sources, but secondary nonetheless. The information there will provide a great starting point for additional research.

Photos

Some of my most prized possessions are old photos of my family, and they can yield a wealth of genealogical information, especially if whoever owned them took the time to write on the backs of the pictures. Family photos tipped me off to sons and daughters that I hadn't known existed before I had the picture.

Old photos can also provide clues to help you in your research. Many of the photos I have include the name of the photo gallery they were taken at, and the town of the gallery. While that isn't a guarantee that the family lived there (perhaps they were in town visiting a relative or attending the County Fair), it will likely at least let you know that they lived nearby. An old multi-generation photo that has the date written on the back might indicate that your 2nd great grandfather was still alive at the time the photo was taken, but that a similar family picture taken two years later is missing him, but includes his wife. That gives you a two-year window in which to look for your 2nd great grandfather's death date.

On a personal note, I like to study the fashions in the photos - the clothes, hairdos, brooches, necklaces, pocket watches, etc. I especially like to see what kind of shoes the individuals were wearing. For example, I noticed that in many of my old family pictures, even though the family was dressed in their Sunday-go-to-meeting clothes, they were often wearing old, worn-out work shoes.

Old Legal Papers

I have learned that many older relatives were pack rats and kept many things - old letters, wills, deeds, etc. These too can provide a wealth of information for beginning (and advanced) genealogists. Whether you find them in the possession of your great Aunt Ruth or on a microfilm somewhere, they often provide clues to follow up on.

A will tells you that at least on the date the will was drawn, the individual was still alive! It may also shed light on the names and ages of children, and the married names of some of the daughters. You'll know where they lived at the time the will was drawn, and may even learn of the location of married children. One entry I recall said something like, "...and to my daughter Emma Adelia Sellers Cunningham of Vinita, Oklahoma, I leave...." Other clues are not so obvious. Wills always needed two witnesses, and those witnesses were often members of the family. I have seen wills witnessed by sons-in-law, fathers of sons-in law, brothers and children.

Deeds also provide information about where the family lived, and their relative prosperity at that time in their life. I have been amazed at how many times land changed hands between others, parents and children, in-laws, etc. Of course these relationships aren't always listed on the deeds, but they give us another clue to follow up on. If I found that my great grandfather Jeremiah Hudson had sold some land to a James Dallas Hudson, you'd better believe that I would make a note of that and try to find out just who this James Dallas Hudson was, and what (if any) his relationship was to Jeremiah (and to me).

Family Histories/Genealogies

Sometimes you may run across a family history that has been written - either specifically about your family or about a family that one of your ancestors married in to. They are incredible finds, often containing hundreds if not thousands of names. But remember, the information contained in books such as these should be considered as coming from secondary sources, not primary. In my experience, few of these books, especially those written many years ago, contain any sort of citations indicating where the information came from. From personal experience I can tell you they are great sources of leads, but the information is often erroneous. Be grateful to those who compiled them, but use them wisely.

More Than A Coin Collection

Most genealogists will tell you that genealogy is more than just collecting names. It is learning about each individual and discovering (and appreciating) their role in life and history.

As I research, I often find myself vicariously living the lives of those whom I am researching. I remember spending time with family members in the Virginia State Library. Poring over their vital records there, I found many of my ancestors. I recall vividly my feelings about one particular family. I sorrowed with them as I learned about the scalding death of their oldest child when he was 20 months old. I rejoiced at the birth of his brother sometime later, only to be dismayed at his death only 22 months later. Again, I rejoiced at the birth of another brother but was crushed to learn shortly thereafter of his death when he was 22 months old. My joy at the birth of a fourth son was tempered, fearing the worst for this family. Imagine my joy when I found records that told of his marriage - he had survived childhood.

At the time of this experience, one of my own children was 24 months old. I remember how painful it was to think of losing her at that age, as this family had lost their precious little ones time after time after time. I wept with them, and then wept again. Finally I wept tears of joy. I remember thinking how nervous the parents must have been as they approached this last son's 18-month birthday, then his 20-month birthday, and finally his 24-month birthday. I could imagine the figurative sigh of relief and the lessening anxiety as this son put distance between himself and his 2nd birthday and grew to manhood.

I used to teach genealogy classes to university students. In my first class, I would bring in a page torn randomly from the local white pages. I tried to impress upon them the fact that with this random act, I could learn more about total strangers than they probably knew about their own great grandparents. In addition to knowing the strangers' addresses and telephone numbers, I could also discover their profession, such as real estate agent, attorney, doctor, etc. I could often tell if they had children, and the approximate age of at least one of those children (through the "teen line" white pages entry). On more than a few, I could even tell whether they were married - and I knew their spouse's name.

How about you? Can you pass that test? Do you learn more about total strangers than the ancestors who contributed your red hair or analytical mind?

Getting Started Checklist

___ What do you already know? Write it down!

___ Gather all the materials you already have – birth, marriage and death certificates, miscellaneous memorabilia, etc.

___ Identify relatives that might know genealogical information about the family.

___ Arrange to interview family members who may be able to share information about the family.

___ Be prepared during interviews: audio or video recorder, paper, pencil, etc.

___ Keep good notes of all research you do, including date, source, place of research, etc.

___ Get copies of government documents, photos, etc.

Additional Resources

Curtiss, Richard D., Gary L. Shumway, Sharon Stephenson, *A Guide for Oral History Programs,* California State University, Fullerton (June 1973).

Mills, Elizabeth Shown, *Evidence!: Citation & Analysis for the Family Historian,* Genealogical Publishing Company (January 2000).

Schull, Wilma Sadler, *Photographing Your Heritage*, Ancestry Publishing (April 1988).

Wright, Norman Edgar, *Preserving Your American Heritage: A Guide to Family and Local History,* Brigham Young University Press (June 1981).

4. Get Organized

Before you get too far in your genealogical quest, it is wise to develop some way to organize your genealogy. When you are first beginning, your organization will probably be like mine was – very simple. But it will amaze you (it did me!) just how quickly you will amass volumes of papers, notes, photos, documents, etc. A good system of organization will help you keep it all straight and enable you to find information whenever you need to. In the last chapter, we talked about collecting various and sundry genealogical documents: birth, baptismal, marriage and death certificates, awards, etc. Once you have collected them, you'll want a way to keep them safe and a way to find them easily.

There are two kinds of organization: for information you have found, and for information you are searching for. Here are the basics of both:

Information You Have Found

I suggest setting up a simple filing system as you get started. If you keep it simple and do it right, you can expand it as you go, keeping the same basic organizational foundations. I tried several kinds of systems when I began my research, and this one worked best for me. Here are the materials you'll need:

• File cabinet or file box
• Tabbed manila folders
• Three-ring notebook
• Hanging folders
• Tabs for the hanging folders

If you cannot afford or do not have enough room for a filing cabinet, you can get file boxes at your local K-Mart, WalMart or Target pretty inexpensively, and they serve the same purpose. The hanging file folders are an important part of your organization, whether you use a file cabinet or file box.

Begin by writing down all the surnames (last names) of the families you know you will be doing research for. Initially, this will be a small number, but will grow more rapidly than you will believe. Always use the maiden names of the women in your family tree. Start with all the surnames you are familiar with: your surname, your spouse's, your father's and mother's surnames, your grandparents' surnames, etc. After you have identified these names, put one surname on a small slip of tag-board that will fit into the tabs for each hanging folder. After you have completed each surname, slide it into a clear tab, and then attach it to one of the hanging file folders.

Using the surnames of my family who were "introduced" in the first chapter, I would set up files for the following families:

Burke	Peoples
Crawford	Phillips
Cunningham	Quillen
Graham	Ritchey
Duvall	Rogers
Horney	Sellers
Hudson	Stunkard
Lowrance	Throckmorton
McClure	Turpin
McCollough	

Now take the manila folders and on the small protruding tab, write the following labels:

• Birth
• Correspondence
• Death
• Marriage
• Other records
• Photographs

Each of these files will hold information that is important for the surname you are researching.

Birth, Death and Marriage Records

This is the place where you will store all records that you come across that provide birth, death or marriage information for the surname you are researching. Initially, it is not important to separate various generations or families. As I work on the Hudson family, for example, I will file all the birth certificates I find for Hudson family members in this one manila folder, which will be contained in the "Hudson" file.

I would include here any birth, death or marriage records you receive, governmental or otherwise. Official birth, death and marriage certificates go here, of course, but I would also include copies of the center section of a family Bible, a handwritten note for the file that indicated Aunt Ruth said Uncle Creed was born on such-and-such a date, etc. With the inexpensive cost of photocopying these days, I would also include the copy of a death certificate in the birth folder if it listed a birth date on it, even though the death certificate also will be in the manila folder marked *Death* in the file. As the file gets full, I might consolidate this kind of duplicate information, but while starting out I would include it.

Since you will be keeping multiple generations of records here, I would file them alphabetically by first name (since all the records in this file will have the same last name).

Correspondence

Although research on the Internet has significantly cut down the amount of correspondence I have, I still have enough to justify a manila folder for correspondence. Here I keep copies of letters and e-mails I have sent out, and responses that I receive.

When you receive a response to an inquiry you have sent – whether full of information or indicating that nothing was found for the particular request – always attach the response to the inquiry. I can tell you from personal experience how frustrating it is months or years later to find a response in a pile of papers, and not know where it came from or what information was originally requested.

Other Records

Include here the other miscellaneous and sundry records that you discover that are of genealogical significance. Copies of wills, deeds, land records, military records, etc. are examples of records that might go in this file. If you find that you are collecting a lot of wills, then by all means start another manila folder titled *Wills*. But until you receive a sufficient volume of wills to justify that, I would use the *Other Records* file for them.

Photographs

Not all of the photographs I have end up in albums, although more than a few do. These might be photos of your great grandfather's hometown, or the old homestead. They may also be photos of tombstones and other interesting tidbits of genealogical interest. They may also be old family photos your mother or grandmother has reluctantly parted with.

Information for Which You Are Searching

Now let's discuss organization as it relates to information you are searching for. Let me share one of the biggest mistakes I made when I first began doing genealogy. Had I been able to avoid this mistake, I would have saved myself countless hours of research that covered ground I had already scoured. I hope you learn from my mistake, and don't make it yourself.

Remember these three words: *Write it down!* When you are doing research, write down the sources you are searching. Write down the date you made your search. It doesn't really matter where you write it down, just put it down somewhere!

Write it down — no matter what the source, write it down. At the time of your research, you'll think that you'll always remember where you got your information, but that may well not be the case five months (or five years!) from now. And if you end up with conflicting dates or places, it will be important to know (and have documented!) whether the source was Aunt Ruth's memory or the birth certificate in someone else's possession.

Forms

Purchasing or creating forms are some of the easiest ways of keeping you on track when you are researching. First of all, spaces on the forms remind you to look for specific information. They help keep you organized in your research. Also, a good form will give you loads of genealogical information at a glance.

You may purchase genealogical forms in a variety of places. The **Church of Jesus Christ of Latter-day Saints** is one of the premier genealogical organizations in the world, and they have well-designed forms available on their website (www.familysearch.org) or from their Distribution Center in Salt Lake City, Utah (Tel. 800/537-5950). See Chapter 10 for more information on the LDS Church as a resource for genealogy work. The **National Genealogical Society** also has a variety of forms available, and these are also pretty inexpensive. Their mailing address is 4527 17th Street, Arlington, Virginia 22207-2363.

Following are a few forms that will assist you in your research.

Research Log

The Research Log will help you keep track of the sources you have searched while looking for information on one of your ancestors. It is a simple form designed to keep you from scouring the same records in search of the same information.

In the example on the next page, I have entered some information dealing with the search for my great grandfather's birth date.

RESEARCH LOG

Ancestor's Given Name(s): EDGAR ESTIL   Last name: QUILLEN   Page 1 of ___

Research Objective: FIND GRANDPA ED'S BIRTHDAY. HE ALWAYS SAID HE WAS BORN 15 JAN 1880, BUT THE 1880 CENSUS (WHICH WAS TAKEN JUNE 1, 1880) LISTS EVERYONE IN HIS FAMILY - EXCEPT HIM. SO I THINK HE MAY HAVE BEEN BORN AFTER THE CENSUS WAS TAKEN.

Date of Search	Source:	Comments
9 Dec 1998	1880 LEE CO. VIRGINIA CENSUS	ALL THE FAMILY BUT GRANDPA ED ARE THERE - CENSUS DATE 1 JUNE 1880.
3 Aug 1999	LEE COUNTY VIRGINIA RECORDS, BOOK IN GATE CITY, VA.	GRANDPA ED's BIRTH INFO IS NOT RECORDED, ALTHOUGH HIS BROTHERS AND SISTERS ARE.
6 Aug 1999	VIRGINIA STATE LIBRARY - VITAL STATISTICS SECTION	I WENT THROUGH 20 YEARS OF BIRTH RECORDS FOR LEE CO AND THERE IS NO RECORD OF HIS BIRTH.
7 Jan 2001	FAMILYSEARCH.ORG	CHECKED RECORDS ON FAMILYSEARCH.ORG, BUT THERE WERE NO RECORDS OF HIS BIRTH THERE.

Family Group Sheet

One of the most helpful forms you'll use in your genealogical research is the Family Group Sheet. It will become central to your work, as it helps you group individuals into family groups. Once completed, it provides one-stop shopping for a great deal of family history information.

The top portion of the Family Group Sheet contains spaces for critical information about the husband and wife of the family you are researching. The following information can be collected for each:

• Birth dates and places
• Death dates and places
• Burial dates and places
• Marriage date and place
• Spouse's name
• Name of the father and mother of the husband and wife

Since everyone is someone's child, if you know the father or mother of the husband or wife, you've already got a start on the Family Group Sheet for the next generation. The *Father* from this group sheet becomes the *Husband* on the next Family Group sheet, and the *Husband* on this Family Group sheet becomes one of the children on his father's Group Sheet (got that?!).

After you have completed all the information you have for the husband and wife of this family, below them is the section for the children. You'll have the opportunity to complete basically the same information for them as you did for their parents.

As an example, I have completed the form below for my second great grandfather's family. As you can see, the form begins with Jonathan Baldwin Quillen and his wife Sarah Minerva Burke. You may note as you scan the information that I have many holes in my research. Death dates are missing for most of my 2nd great grandfather's children, and I haven't yet found information about most of his children's marriages.

In the top right-hand corner of the form you'll note that this is the first of two pages. That tells you this is a partial listing of my 2nd great grandfather's family – he had nine children, and this form only has room for six of them. The three youngest children are included on another Family Group Sheet.

RESEARCH NOTE ON SURNAMES

Family history is a bit old fashioned (is it redundant to say genealogy is old fashioned?): information about families is found and recorded under the male surname.

Take a look at the front and back pages of the group sheet and familiarize yourself with them. Note that each informational entry has a space to the far right of the line labeled *Source: # X* (where *X* is actually a number). This refers to the line on the back of the Family Group sheet that provides you with the opportunity to cite where the information came from for this particular bit of information. This is a critical aspect of efficient genealogical research; ignore it or be sloppy about it and I promise you will curse yourself later on. Just get into the habit of keeping track of where you got your information and your research will be a lot easier for you.

It is important for you to provide accurate and complete citation information for each bit of data that you have. If more than one source was used for birth date and place information, then each source should be cited. For example, in the case of my 2nd great grandfather, we "know" that he was born in Sullivan, Hawkins County, Tennessee because that is what he told his granddaughter (my great Aunt Ruth). We have estimated his birth date based on the 1870 and 1880 censuses, which list his age as 25 and 35 years old, respectively (1870 – 25 = 1845, and 1880 – 35 = 1845). If we find better sources later (like a birth certificate), we'll change it on the forms.

Note that the dates are listed as day, month (with month listed by the first three letters of the month), and full year. (Using the full year instead of two digit years helps keep ancestors in the right century!) As you do genealogical research, you'll see a variety of formats for dates, but the most common format for genealogists is day, month, and year. Get into the habit of listing dates – at least when doing genealogy – in that manner. If you are not faithful to any particular format, you may find yourself later wondering whether 6/1/ 1903 is 6 January 1903 or June 1, 1903! 6 Jan 1903 is pretty clear and understandable by you and anyone with whom you share your genealogy.

If you would like an electronic copy of any of these forms, just e-mail me at the e-mail address contained in one of the first few pages of this book, and I will be happy to send you electronic copies of the forms. If you have the electronic versions of the forms, you can put them on your computer and complete them on the computer, using hard copy as your research copies, then transferring the information to the computer.

Alternately, you may purchase forms from a variety of locations and genealogical societies. Most contain basically the same information, but it may be arranged a little differently on each form. Just pick a form that works best for you.

FAMILY GROUP SHEET

Husband		Page 1 of 2	
Given name(s): Jonathan Baldwin		Last name: Quillen	
Birth date: Abt 1845	Place: Sullivan, Hawkins Co., Tenn.		Source: # 1
Died: 28 Sep 1921	Place: Hartville, Missouri		Source: # 2
Buried:	Place: Hartville, Missouri		Source: # 3
Married: 28 Sep 1870	Place: Jonesville, Lee, Virginia		Source: # 4
Husband's Father: Charles Franklin		Last name: Quillen	
Husband's Mother: Susan or Susannah		Maiden name:	
Wife			
Given name(s): Sarah Minerva		Maiden name: Burke	
Birth date: Abt 1846	Place: Gate City, Lee Co., Virginia		Source: # 5
Died: 22 Sep 1933	Place: Hartville, Missouri		Source: # 6
Buried:	Place: Hartville, Missouri		Source: # 7
Wife's Father's Given name(s):			
Wife's Mother's Given name(s):			
**************Children – List all children in order of their birth*************			
1. M Given name(s): Emmett Vance		Last name: Quillen	
Birth date: 12 Dec 1870	Place: Gate City, Lee Co., Va		Source: # 8
Died: 26 Dec 1948	Place:		Source: # 9
Married:	Place:		Source: # 10
Spouse's Given name(s):		Last name:	
2. M Given name(s): Thomas Franklin		Last name: Quillen	
Birth date: 18 Jan 1872	Place: Gate City, Lee Co., Va.		Source: # 11
Died: Abt 5 June 1950	Place:		Source: # 12
Married: 7 Jan 1877	Place: Lee Co., Va.		Source: # 13
Spouse Given name(s):		Last name:	
3. F Given name(s): Cora Belle		Last name: Quillen	
Birth date: Abt 1874	Place: Gate City, Lee Co. Va.		Source: # 14
Died:	Died:		Source: # 15
Married:	Place:		Source: # 16
Spouse Given name(s):		Last name:	
4. F Given name(s): Lizzie Leticia		Last name: Quillen	
Birth date: 3 Apr 1877	Place: Nashville, Davidson, Tenn.		Source: # 17
Died:	Place:		Source: # 18
Married:	Place:		Source: # 19
Spouse Given name(s):		Last name:	
5. M Given name(s): William Evan		Last name: Quillen	
Birth date: 15 Oct 1878	Place: Gate City, Lee Co., Va.		Source: # 20
Died: 4 Oct 1869	Place:		Source: # 21
Married:	Place:		Source: # 22
Spouse Given name(s):		Last name:	
6. M Given name(s): Edgar Estil		Last name: Quillen	
Birth date: 15 Jan 1881?	Place: Gate City, Lee, Va.		Source: # 23
Died: 6 May 1978	Place: Ralston, OK		Source: # 24
Married: 18 Mar 1904	Place: Ralston, OK		Source: # 25
Spouse Given name(s): Theodora Charity		Last name: McCollough	

FAMILY GROUP SHEET

Source List

#1. Place is from family tradition; from Ruth Wedd, granddaughter. Birth date is estimated from 1870 and 1880 Censuses for Lee Co., Virginia

#2. Family tradition; from Ruth Wedd, granddaughter

#3. Family tradition; from Ruth Wedd, granddaughter

#4. Lee Co, Virginia Marriage Registry, located in Gate City, Virginia. Page 203

#5. Lee Co. Birth Registry, on microfilm at the Virginia State Library in Richmond

#6. Family tradition; from Ruth Wedd, grandaughter

#7. Family tradition; from Ruth Wedd, granddaughter

#8. Record of birth in possession of Daniel Quillen

#9. Record of birth in possession of Daniel Quillen

#10.

#11. Record of birth in possession of Daniel Quillen

#12.

#13. Lee Co. Marriage Registry, on microfilm at the Virginia State Library in Richmond

#14. Family tradition; from Ruth Wedd.

#15.

#16.

#17. Record of Birth in possession of Daniel Quillen

#18.

#19.

#20. Record of Birth in possession of Daniel Quillen

#21. Ruth Wedd

#22.

#23. Personal knowledge (?) of Ed Quillen. Question comes from 1880 Census of Lee Co.

#24. Ruth Wedd

#25. Marriage certificate in possession of Ruth Wedd

Pedigree Charts

Pedigree charts are line charts that show at a glance an individual's direct ancestors (pedigree charts are sometimes referred to as *Ascendancy Charts*). Beginning at the left-hand side of the chart, you'll find one individual. To his or her right, and a little above and below you'll find his/her parents. Fathers are always listed above the mothers.

In the first chapter of this book, I introduced my family. If you go back to that listing, you'll note that the pedigree chart provides the same information (and more!) in a much more convenient – and informative - format.

As useful as pedigree charts are for seeing a flow of ancestors quickly, they have limited value from a research perspective. First of all, while they do list basic information (birth date and place, death date and place, marriage date and place), they do not list sources for that information. Nor do they list children of the marriage, other than the individual immediately to their left.

Most pedigree charts you come across show four or five generations, and these are best to aid you in your research. Larger, mostly wall-style charts list a dozen or more generations.

If you look on the following page, you'll see a Pedigree Chart beginning with my paternal grandfather.

Use the three-ring binder I mentioned early in this chapter to store your Family Group sheets, Research Logs and Pedigree charts. Set up with tabs for each surname you are researching. As you complete each Family Group sheet or pedigree chart, file it under the appropriate tab, and do so sequentially, from one generation to the next. Eventually you may need a notebook for each surname, but to begin with it is okay to combine them all in one notebook.

Get Organized Checklist

____ Gather together all the information you have found – certificates, photos, etc.

____ Decide on an organizational methodology (file cabinet, binders, etc.)

____ Procure materials that will support your method of organization.

____ As you gather information, write it down and then file it!

____ Familiarize yourself with forms that may assist you in organizing the genealogical information you collect.

____ Select the appropriate forms you need to match the information you have.

Pedigree Chart

Number 1 is the same as number ___ on chart number ___

Chart number ___

8. Charles Franklin Quillen
Father of #4
Born: Abt 1826   Place: Stokes Co, NC
Mar: Abt 1844   Place:
Died: Place:

4. Jonathan Baldwin Quillen
Father of #2
Born: Abt. 1845   Place: Sullivan Co, TN (?)
Mar: 28 Sep 1870   Place: Jonesville, Lee, VA
Died: 28 Sep 1921 Place:Hartville, MO

9. Susan or Susannah
Mother of #4
Born: Place:
Died: Place:

2. Edgar Estil Quillen
Father of #1
Born: 15 Jan 1881(?) Place: Lee Co. VA (?)
Mar: 18 Mar 1904   Place: Ralston, OK
Died: 6 May 1978   Place: Fairfax, OK

10. _____
Father of #5
Born: Place:
Mar: Place:
Died: Place:

5. Sarah Minerva Burke
Mother of #2
Born: Abt. 1846   Place: Lee Co, VA (?)
Died: 22 Sep 1932/33 Place: Hartville, MO

11. _____
Mother of #5
Born: Place:
Died: Place:

1. Helon Edgar Quillen
Born: 18 Jan 1906   Place: Ralston, Pawnee, OK
Mar: 26 May 1928   Place: Ralston, Oklahoma
Died: 6 May 1978   Place: Fairfax, Osage, OK

Spouse of # 1 **Vivian Iris Cunningham**

12. Samuel McCollough
Father of #6
Born: 10 Feb 1837   Place: of Bristoria, PA
Mar: 3 Mar 1856   Place: Waynesburg, PA
Died: 22 Feb 1871   Place: Waynesburg, PA

6. William L. McCollough
Father of #3
Born: 16 Jul 1862   Place: of Bristoria, PA
Mar: 19 Aug 1883   Place: Waynesburg, PA
Died: 9 May 1927   Place: Ralston, OK

13. Elizabeth Throckmorton
Mother of #6
Born: 1 Nov 1835   Place: Waynesburg, PA
Died: 25 Dec 1913   Place: Rymer, WVA

3. Theodora Charity McCollough
Mother of #1
Born: 22 Sep 1884   Place: Waynesburg, PA
Died: 3 Dec 1971   Place: Fairfax, OK

14. Oliver Sayers Phillips
Father of #7
Born: 21 Aug 1829   Place: Prosperity, PA
Mar: 1 Aug 1849   Place: Greene, PA
Died: 17 Mar 1899   Place: Greene, PA

7. Lucy Arabella Phillips
Mother of #3
Born: 20 Jun 1860   Place: Waynesburg, PA
Died: 18 Jun 1948   Place: Ralston, OK

15. Charity Graham
Mother of #7
Born: 16 Aug 1833   Place: Center Twp., PA
Died: Place:

Additional Resources

Carmack, Sharon Debartolo, *Organizing Your Family History Search: Efficient & Effective Ways to Gather and Protect Your Genealogical Research*, Betterway Publications. (April 1999)

Carmichael, David, *Organizing Archival Records: A Practical Method of Arrangement*, Pennsylvania Historical Society. (February 1993)

Dollarhide, William, *Managing a Genealogical Project*, Genealogical Publishing Company. (May 1999)

Lackey, Richard S., *Cite Your Sources: A Manual for Documenting Family Histories and Genealogical Records*, University Press of Mississippi. (February 1986)

5. What's in a Name?

When I was growing up, one of my classmates was named Eric, and he had copper-colored bright red hair. On one occasion, our sixth grade class was covering a unit on family history and we were each asked to find out about one of our ancestors, and prepare and present an oral report to the class. When the day came for Eric to make his report, he stood in front of the class, blushing to the tips of his ears, and told us that one of his ancestors was Eric the Red, the intrepid Viking explorer....(yeah, right Eric!). As I recall, we had a pretty good laugh at Eric's expense. I never did find out whether he was kidding us or not.

Then again, maybe he wasn't kidding; little did I know then, but through the centuries, many people were named after physical characteristics that they or a relative possessed. In fact, there is a wide variety of naming schemes that might give you a clue to something about your progenitors. Read on for a few thoughts on the topic.

Physical Characteristics

Many of those around us still carry the names of our progenitors that may have once reflected their physical characteristics. Ever know a person whose surname was Klein? Klein means small in German. How about Rubio (Spanish for blonde) or Blanco (Spanish for white)? Delgado means thin in Spanish, and the popular name Rojas may have been once used to identify a strain of the family with red hair (since rojas means red or rosy).

An Animal Connection

Many surnames reflect the names of animals. Perhaps an ancestor handled, raised or sold certain kinds of animals, or perhaps they were just fond of or admired a particular kind of animal. They may have even looked like a particular animal. Consider for example, the following: *Adler* (eagle in

German), *Aguilar* (eagle in Spanish), *Haas* (rabbit in German) or *Garcia* (fox in Spanish) or *Fox* (also fox in English). Have you ever known someone named *Leon* (lion in Spanish) or perhaps *Faulkner* (falken is hawk in German)?

Patronymics

Many cultures employed the use of patronymics when taking names for themselves. A patronymic is a name that identifies the named person with his or her father.

The Irish had their own form of patronymics recognized the world over. Prefixes such as Mc or Mac were used to signify the *son of*: McDonnell was therefore the son of Donell. Another prefix was the O' which meant "descended from," and a grandson or great grandson might use such a prefix. Occasionally the English passed laws to annoy the Irish (actually, they were trying to assimilate them into English culture). One such law forbade the use of the patronymics O' and Mc. At that time, the patronymic *fitz* replaced *Mc* for son of: Fitzmorris then meant the son of Morris.

Almost as prevalent as Irish patronymics are Scandinavian patronymics. I suppose we all know more than our fair share of individuals with surnames like Anderson (Anders' son) and Johnson (John's son). For centuries Scandinavians employed this naming scheme, and until surnames became common (in the late 1700s or early 1800s depending on the location), the names changed from generation to generation.

The Jewish culture also has its patronymics. You will occasionally see the name *ben* used to designate the son of, as in David *ben* Joseph (David, the son of Joseph). Certain Jewish groups also used patronymics to honor living grandparents, and there was a specific order used to designate names. The first-born son was often named after his paternal grandfather, and his brother (the second son) was named after his maternal grandfather. They used this practice for their daughters too: first-born daughters were given the name of their paternal grandmother and second-born daughters received the names of their maternal grandmother. This method of naming was especially popular with Sephardic Jews.

The French adopted the term fitz to mean son of: Fitzpatrick was therefore the son of Patrick (fitz was derived from the French work fils, which means son).

Spanish surnames are often derived from patronymics. In Spain and Portugal, an abbreviated way to identify a person with his or her father was by the addition of az, ez, iz, or oz to their father's last name. For instance, Julio, el hijo de Rodrigo became Julio Rodriquez (Julio, the son of Rodrigo).

And let's not forget that the Russians also used patronymics. It was common for Russians to have as their middle name the name of their father, with a –vitch added for the sons or –evna or -ovna added for their daughters. If I may borrow from author Leo Tolstoy's epic novel *Anna Karenina*, I will give you a few examples to illustrate this. The main character in the novel is Anna Arkadyevna Karenina – Anna, the daughter of Arkady. Her brother is Stepan Arkadyevich Oblonsky – Stepan, the son of Arkady. Konstantin Dmitrievitch Levin (Konstantin, son of Dmitri) was enamored with Anna's sister-in-law: Katarina Alexandrovna Oblonsky (Katarina, daughter of Alexandr), and Anna's lover was Alexey Kirillovitch Vronsky (Alexey, the son of Kirill), much to the dismay of her husband, Alexey Alexandrovitch Karenin (Alexey, the son of Alexandr). Phew!

While that may seem overwhelming, your Russian ancestors' very names may well contain clues to their next generation by providing their father's name.

DON'T DO IT!

I can almost guarantee you that at some time or other in your research you will run across information that you'll "know" just isn't right. The temptation will be to correct the information rather than just write down what you have found.

Don't do it!

Perhaps it's the first name of an ancestor. While you might be absolutely certain that your great great grandmother's name is Theodora, if you find her listed in a US Census as "Dolly," that is the name you should record as you copy the data down. Or perhaps it's your last name that has been spelled creatively. Resist the temptation to substitute the information that is different. Copy the record exactly as you find it so that you can have an accurate representation of what you found.

Occupations

I suppose like most Americans, throughout your lifetime you have known many individuals named Miller, Smith, Carpenter, Carver, Schneider, Guerrero and Escobedo. Each of these surnames may be indicative that an ancestor owned or worked at a mill (Miller), was a blacksmith (Smith), built things (Carpenter), was one who carved (Carver), earned his keep as a tailor (Schneider means tailor in German), a soldier (Guerrero means soldier or warrior in Spanish) or worked as a sweeper (Escobedo).

How about names like Joiner (construction term), or Metzger (German for butcher). I've a friend whose mother's maiden name was Kirchebauer – German for church builder. My friend Karl Fischer might be descended from a man who fished for a living (since fisch is the German name for fish). Do you suppose you can figure out the occupation of at least one of the Weaver ancestors?

Geographic Locations

Don't overlook the possibility that your surname is derived from a town, country, or physical geographic attribute associated with an ancestor. I once had two roommates named Mike. We called one Mike Jersey because he was from New Jersey. The concept is the same. Let's say there were two Mikes who lived near the same village several hundred years ago, before surnames were common. One lived by a lake, and the other at the foot of a hill. They might have been called Mike Lake and Mike Hill, respectively. I had a friend named Duane Alleman once, and I'd be willing to bet at least one of his paternal ancestors was German (Alemán is the Spanish word for German) who lived someplace where Spanish was spoken. Or how many people are you acquainted with who have the surname French? I'd wager somewhere in their family tree is a French ancestor.

As you climb your family tree, it is fun to be aware of these things – it just adds another element to your detective work.

Mother's Maiden Names

Another fairly common naming custom has been the use of the mother's maiden name by one or more of her sons. I was once doing research on one of my family lines, and I came across a fellow named Hartle Hart Sellers. I wondered if Hart might not be his mother's maiden name, and sure enough, after much research, I found that Hart was indeed her maiden name. Again, a genealogical clue right in the midst of your ancestor's name!

Don't Assume...

As you are doing your research, don't fall into the trap that I once fell into. As a relatively inexperienced genealogist, I was doing research in central Pennsylvania. I was scouring the 1880 US Census, and discovered that one of my ancestors had married a young woman by the name of Mahalia. What an interesting – and unique! – name that was. To determine her maiden name, I decided to search the 1870 US Census, when she would have been 11 or 12 years old. I reasoned that if I could find an 11- or 12-year-old girl named Mahalia in one of the families in that county, I would probably have found her maiden name, since Mahalia was such an odd name.

Sure enough, after just a little bit of searching, I found a Mahalia listed with her family not far from my own family on the census. I happily penned her maiden name on my forms and went merrily on my way.

It wasn't until years later when I was doing additional research in that same county that I discovered that contrary to my assumption, Mahalia was a very common name in 1870 Pennsylvania! Further research into other records proved the fallacy of my earlier assumption about her maiden name.

Another example – my brother-in-law had a great-great uncle named Adam. Adam died as a little boy. The next son born to that same family was named Adam after his older brother. He also died. Finally, a third son was born to the same family, and he too was named Adam. This Adam lived, but as my brother-in-law did his research, he had to be careful to get the right birthdate for the right Adam!

Spelling Woes

Here's a hint that is probably heresy to my 6th grade teacher: Don't limit yourself to only one spelling of your name. In my research, in nearly every one of my family lines, at one time or another I have found variations in the spelling – sometimes within the same generation! Here are a few examples from my own family:

- Sellers, Sellars, Sellar
- Ritchie, Ritchey, Richey
- Horney, Harney
- Quillan, Quillen, Quillon, Quillin, McQuillan, McQuillon, etc.
- Lowrance/Lorentz
- McCollough/McCullough
- Rogers/Rodgers
- Throckmorton, Throgmorton
- Hudson/Hutson
- Graham/Grimes

And just because you are a Smith or a Jones (by the way - is it true that the surname of Adam and Eve was Jones?), don't assume you are immune from spelling changes: Smith/Smythe/Smithy/Schmidt or Jones/Jonas/ Joans, etc.

There are many reasons for this, and your creative detective work will have to gather all the threads together into one cohesive answer. Immigration officials are often accused of this, but in my opinion that happened far less than was alleged. It may have been an immigration official, or it may have been illiteracy. The spelling of my surname may be an example of the latter. The family tradition is that several generations of my farming ancestors saw no use in sending their children to school. When the first kids in 75 years went to the local one-room schoolhouse, the teacher asked how they spelled their last name (the correct spelling was Quillan). The children responded that they didn't know, so the teacher "taught" them how to spell it: Quillen. No one at home knew better, so the spelling is the one my line of the family uses today. True story or false? I don't know, but I have seen family members' names spelled differently on US Censuses, marriage licenses, birth certificates, etc.

Another reason might be that a newly immigrated family wanted to fit in to their newly adopted country. In that case, Meier became Meyer, Schneider became Snider, Schmidt became Smith and Blau became Blue. In my family, McQuillan became Quillan.

What's in a Name? Checklist

___ Write down all the possible spellings you can think of for the surname you are researching.

___ Don't ignore surnames that are similar to but spelled differently than the one you are researching.

___ Look for clues in your name that might indicate where an ancestor was born, or might indicate a possible occupational clue.

___ Watch for patronymics and learn how to use them to help you in your ancestral search.

___ If you come across a name that is spelled differently than how you think it should be spelled, write it down exactly as it appears in the research record.

___ Because a name sounds strange or odd to your 21st-century ears, that doesn't mean it wasn't very common in the era or area where you are researching.

___ Watch for middle names that might give a clue to a mother's maiden name.

Additional Resources
Rose, Christine, *Nicknames: Past and Present*, Rose Family Association, 3rd edition. (May 1998)

6. Vital Records

Vital records are those records that are critical to successful and accurate genealogical research. They are quite frankly the goal every genealogical researcher should strive to achieve for each ancestor they are researching. They are original records that provide information about the names, dates and places of births, marriages and deaths of those for whom you are searching.

These important and original records will often shed a great deal of light on the family you are researching. I have seen birth certificates, for example, that contain some or all of the following information:

• Individual's full name
• Birth date
• Place of birth
• Residence of parents (if different than birthplace)
• Mother's full maiden name
• Mother's age at the time of this birth
• Number of children born previously to this mother
• Father's full name
• Father's age at the time of this birth
• Father's occupation
• State or country of origin of parents

Death certificates likewise contain some of the same information, adding the death date, cause of death and the spouse's name. Marriage certificates often provide just the basics: full names of the bride and groom and the date and place of the marriage. Marriage registers, however, often contain more information about the couple, including parents' names and the age of the bride and groom. Marriage registers were books that were kept by the local government (typically the county) of all marriages occurring within its boundaries.

Where to Look?

So now that you know what vital records are, where do you go to find them? Bear in mind that entire books have been written on this very topic. One of the most exhaustive and a definite resource to obtain to aid you in your research is George B. Everton's *Handy Book for Genealogists: United States of America*. It is a thorough guide that will help you find just about any type of government record available – federal, state, or county. It covers every type of governmental record conceivable and details time periods those records are available in each jurisdiction. Over 600 pages of incredible detail await you. In addition to providing you with what information is available, it also tells you how to go about getting it: where to write and who to address your letter to.

Each state requires the housing of vital records for their state. Some of these states required those records to be centralized for easier access, while others simply required each county or city to keep the records. That is why a good resource book such as George Everton's *Handy Book for Genealogists: United States of America* is invaluable. It will guide you to the right place the first time. Without a resource like that, you will not know whether to write to the State Department of Vital Records or the local county courthouse where your ancestor was born.

Another option for finding where to write if you are computer literate is to search the Internet for the offices of Vital Records (sometimes called Vital Statistics) for the various states. Ancestry.com has a nice feature that is available without subscription. It lists all the states, their mailing addresses and the websites of their Vital Records departments. It also provides lists of records that are available, and the dates those records are available, along with the cost of copies. The Ancestry.com website is www.vitalrec.com.

Another organization that provides similar information is the National Center for Health Statistics, and their website is *www.cdc.gov/nchs/howto/ w2w/w2welcom.htm*. In addition, most of the states have a similar website. You may find that website by entering *(State name) Department of Vital Records* in your search engine. Alternately, I have provided the addresses, phone numbers and websites of each state's Department of Records at the end of this book in Appendix C. Each entry also lists the cost of birth and death certificates.

What Do I Say?

Writing for information need not be a complicated and drawn-out affair – in fact, it should be very simple. But there are a few "rules" that you should follow when writing to request information:

1. Always include a self-addressed, stamped envelope (SASE) with your request. Use a #10 business envelope.

2. Always include your return address underneath your signature (just like you were taught in school). Letters and envelopes often get separated; this will ensure that the clerk handling your request will have your address.

3. Keep your request simple: don't request fourteen bits of information. For example, request one or two marriage certificates at a time, rather than three marriage certificates, two birth certificates, a death certificate and two wills. You will likely find that your total request will be filled more quickly if you break it up into bite-size pieces.

4. Include payment if you know how much it is. If you do not know the cost, then send a query letter prior to your request asking for the costs. (Note: with today's low long-distance rates, I have found it less expensive – and quicker! – to call for this information.) Your payment should be by personal check or money order – never send cash!

5. Be specific about your request – what are you looking for, when did the event occur, and for whom?

6. If the name (first or last) could have been spelled differently, include that different spelling in your request. Otherwise, a clerk may decide that the record he has for Jonathan B. Quillan does not match the request you sent for a birth certificate for Jon Quillen.

7. Include a date range that you are looking for. Generally try to keep the range to five years or less.

8. Include other data that may help the clerk find the right record (parents' names, where you believe the event occurred, cemetery they were buried in, etc.).

Here's a sample letter requesting information about my great grandfather:

> March 15, 2003
> Virginia Office of Vital Records
> P.O. 1000, Richmond, VA 23218-1000
>
> Dear Vital Records Department,
>
> I would like to request a photocopy of the birth certificate of my great grandfather, **Edgar Estil Quillen** (may also be spelled Quillan, Quillon, Quillin). I believe he was born in Lee County between 1879 and 1882. His parents were Jonathan Baldwin Quillen and Sarah Minerva Burke. I have enclosed $10.00 for the birth certificate search, as your website indicates that is the cost. I have also enclosed a SASE for your convenience.
> Thank you, Daniel Quillen

Note that the request is short and sweet and to the point. It is for one request, lists several possible spellings of my great grandfather's last name and provides other information that might help the clerk identify the right record (his parents' names, a range of birth years and the county of his birth). I have also enclosed a check for the correct amount for the birth certificate.

What Do the Records Cost?

The costs for obtaining copies of birth, death and marriage certificates vary from state to state. At the time of this writing, prices range from $4.00 to $15.00, which covers the cost of searches as well as copies of certificates that are found. Most states will not issue a refund if a copy is not found, but will send a letter indicating that a search had been conducted with no success.

Friendly Caution

One caution – always try to discover those records of a person's life that were kept nearest the event. For example, a death certificate might also contain some of the same information as a birth certificate – the person's name, date and place of birth, parents' names, etc. However, that information might have been written down 70 or more years after the event took place, and is likely to be completed by those who were not present at the time. Dimming memories of those who provided the information may have not quite recalled the correct dates or places.

In fact, the information may have been provided by a sibling, cousin or neighbor who never did have quite the exact information. Does that invalidate the information about birth and parentage found in a death certificate? Not necessarily. Just treat it as a clue to assist you in your search for documentation a little closer to the person's birth.

Vital Records Checklist

____ Determine which ancestor you want to get information about.

____ Gather the information you already know about this person (name, place of birth, approximate birth year, etc.)

____ Locate the Vital Records department of the state or county where your ancestor's birth, death or marriage may have taken place. This may be found in Appendix C, on the Internet, or through a book written specifically for this purpose.

____ Write a letter to the state's Vital Records Department, requesting the certificate you are looking for. Make sure to:
____ Include a self-addressed, stamped envelope (SASE)

___ Include a check or money order (never cash!) for the cost of the certificate.

___ Be specific in your request.

___ Do not request too many certificates at one time.

Additional Resources

Bentley, Elizabeth Petty, *The Genealogist's Address Book*, Genealogical Publishing Company. (February 1991)

Dollarhide, William, (Alice Eichholz, editor*), Ancestry's Red Book: American State, County and Town Sources,* Ancestry Publishing. (May 1997)

Everton, George B., *Handy Book for Genealogists: United States of America*, Betterway Publications, 9th edition. (September 1999)

Kemp, Thomas Jay, *International Vital Records Handbook*, Genealogical Publishing Company; (August 1994)

Melnyk, Marcia, *Genealogist's Handbook for New England Research*, New England Historic Genealogical Society, 4th edition. (January 1999)

7. Genealogical Societies

You would expect that any hobby that has as many participants as genealogy does would have many organizations of like-minded people who get together and share their information and expertise. And so it is with genealogy. Literally thousands of genealogical organizations have sprung up through the years in support of this pastime. One or more of them may be just the answer you are looking for to help you find information on your family. And since some of them have been around in one form or another for as much as 150 years, the information they have gleaned on their family lines is often extensive.

A visit to the Internet confirms the existence of these societies, and their willingness to share their information and expertise. The last time I typed "genealogy society" on **Yahoo!** yielded nearly 700 organizations who have websites dedicated to genealogy. Some are area-specific (e.g., Germany, Hancock County, Maine, San Mateo, etc.) and others are family-specific. Some are societies that just provide information, support and expertise to their members. Another source of information on genealogical societies is the **Federation of Genealogical Societies** located at *www.fgs.org*. It boasts over 500,000 members and over 500 family associations and genealogical societies in its membership. By searching for these societies on their website, you can find out about their existence, mail and/or e-mail address, as well any website and telephone numbers that are available.

Membership in most of the genealogical societies is the modest cost of annual dues ($15 to $35 per year). The dues may include access to family or area genealogical information as well as a quarterly newsletter focusing on genealogical aspects of the family or region.

These societies can be of immense assistance to beginning genealogists. Several years ago while doing research for another book, I ran across a list of genealogy societies. Scanning it quickly, I noticed the Hudson Family Association. My grandmother was a Hudson, and despite a number of efforts to learn more about her line, I knew virtually nothing about the family beyond her grandfather. So almost as an afterthought, I jotted down the address, and a few days later I fired off a short letter:

> Dear Hudson Family Association,
>
> I came across your organization in *Moore's Book of Lists*. My grandmother is a Hudson, so I would like to join your organization. The entry in the book didn't have much information about your society, but I am enclosing $50 for dues. If that is too much, please send me as many back issues of your newsletter as the extra amount will purchase.
>
> Thank you,
>
> Daniel Quillen

I am by nature an optimist, so I was cautiously optimistic that the Hudson Family Association would be able to assist me in my Hudson ancestral pursuit. I was totally unprepared for the amount and quality of assistance they gave me.

Within days I received a note welcoming me to the Hudson Family Association. They explained that the association was formed to further genealogical research on the family line, and asked whether I would be willing to share information about my side of the family.

I was happy to share the information (genealogists are like that!) and I shared my information, as scanty as it was. I shared birth and marriage information about my current family, my grandmother, her parents and her paternal grandfather's name and place of birth.

A few weeks later, I received my first copy of the *Bulletin Hudsoniana*, the Hudson Family Association newsletter. One section was devoted to welcoming new members. Imagine my unbounded joy when I found the following entry:

Welcome New Members!
Quillen, W. Daniel:
William Daniel Quillen, born 27 Feb 1956, Lynwood, Los Angeles, CA married 13 April 1979 Bonita BLAU; children: William Michael, Katie Scarlet, Joseph Daniel, Andrew Teague, Emily, Jesse Lee Blaine.

Versie Lee LOWRANCE, born McClain, OK, married 13 July 1951 William Edgar Quillen, born Norman, OK;

Alma HUDSON, born 24 Apr 1913, Stephens, OK, married 5 Oct 1932 Elzie Lee LOWRANCE, born 24 Feb 1906, Wayne, OK;

Francis Marion HUDSON, born 13 Nov 1877, Pope, AR, died 12 Jan 1960, Los Angeles, CA, married 1909 Margaret Ellen TURPIN;

Jeremiah HUDSON, born 1851, AR, died 1914, Dibble, OK, married about 1873 Frances DUVALL, AR;

Francis Marion HUDSON, born 20 March 1829, Lauderdale County, AL, married about 1848 Mary ____;

Jeremiah HUDSON, living 1830 in Lauderdale County, AL, married Lavina JONES, living in 1830 in Lauderdale County, AL;

Levi HUDSON, married Hannah ____;

Major HUDSON, born about 1690, died 16 Nov. 1781, Worchester County, MD, married Martha GILLETT;

Henry HUDSON, born 8 July 1669, Somerset County, Maryland, died 24 Dec 1720, Somerset County, MD married (1) ____ LUDLONG?, (2) Ellis DENNIS;

Henry HUDSON, born about 1642, Accomack County, Virginia, died about 1710, Somerset County, Maryland, married about 1664 Lydia SMITH;

Richard HUDSON, born 1605, England, died about 1657, Northampton County, Virginia, married (1) Mary ____, married (2) Mrs. Mary HAYES, married (3) Barbara JACOBS;

William HUDSON, born about 1570, London, England, married about 1603 Alice Turner;

Henry HUDSON born about 1541

They had taken the scant information I had provided them and tied me back in a direct line of ancestors to 1541 – 13 generations and 450 years! A subsequent request from me provided Family Group Sheets on every family member along with documentation of each name and date – hundreds of names and a great deal of vital statistic information. A wonderful find indeed.

I share this story to assure you that no matter how alone you may feel in your research sometimes, there are often many people out there who have already found the very information you are searching for. And the best part about that message is that they are almost always willing to share that information.

You'll note, by the way, that much of the Hudson family information that was provided to me was unknown, especially the further I climbed the family tree. In a number of instances, there are first names only, or missing dates, or at best approximated dates. That's okay – at least I have information to go on that will help me find some of these people later on.

Genealogy societies provide a variety of valuable services, including:

• Timely how-to advice on research for the family or in a particular area.
• Share, share, share information (that's how I got all that information on the Hudson line).

OLLEY OLLEY OXEN FREE!

Searching for your ancestors is often a little like playing hide-and-go-seek with your four- or five-year-old little brother. He loves the game, but doesn't quite get the rules. Giggling or moving, he seems to delight in being found.

And so it is with many of your ancestors – it seems that often they do all they can to be found. As you work (play!) in genealogy, you'll be surprised at how much information will come to you – almost as though by accident. Through the years I have found that the smallest amount of effort on my part often yields immense genealogical success. Anyone who has done much genealogy at all has multiple stories of amazing coincidences that resulted in genealogical progress – chance meetings with other genealogists working on their line, intuitional feelings leading them to information in least-expected places, etc.

Don't get me wrong – there are still those ancestors out there that seem to be extremely good at playing hide-and-go-seek. Unlike the little brother mentioned at the outset of this section, they are experts at hiding and dodging even your best efforts. They will bring out your best detective instincts! In the mean time, keep looking! If all else fails, try calling, "Olley olley oxen free!" to see if they will reveal their hiding places.

- Preserve and make available records (many societies get involved with microfilming and indexing original records for their members).
- Making your ancestors come alive by providing stories from their lives. Some are humorous, some historical, many are tragic. All serve to help you become better acquainted with your ancestors.
- Recommendations for improving your genealogy research through the announcement (or sponsoring) of seminars or the publication of articles.
- Evaluations of hardware and software used for genealogical purposes.

Genealogical Societies Checklist

____ Determine which surnames you wish to do research on.

____ Seek out websites and books that cover Genealogical Societies.

____ Be prepared to share what you know about your family.

____ Be persistent.

Additional Resources

Meyer, Mary Keysor, *Meyer's Directory of Genealogical Societies in the USA and Canada,* Libra Publications, 9th edition. (May 1992)

Federation of Genealogical Societies website: *www.fgs.org.*

8. Genealogical Collections in Libraries

Thank you, Benjamin Franklin! His idea of public libraries has had many benefits for our society – and especially for genealogists. Many libraries have genealogy sections that are just aching to be searched. A few hours in your local library may yield a surprising amount of genealogical information for you. Whether it is your city library, a national archival center or a small county library, you can often find information that has been buried for years, just waiting to be found.

Family History Library

The Family History Library of the Church of Jesus Christ of Latter-day Saints is indisputably the finest genealogy library in the world. It is so valuable as a resource for genealogists that it has its own separate chapter in this book. Between visits to the library in Salt Lake City, its records that are available through the Internet and its extensive lending library network of over 3,700 Family History Centers (branch offices of the Family History Library), its resources are exceptionally available to individuals no matter where they live. Over 750 million names are in their databases, books and microfilms, and they are all available to genealogists regardless of their religious beliefs.

For more details, be sure and spend some time with the chapter in this book that addresses the Family History Library.

State Libraries

Each state has a major state library, usually located in the state capitol (although not always!). Each of these libraries has a Genealogy section for you to go and search for your ancestors. Depending on the funding the library receives (and has received through the years), their collection may be extensive or somewhat limited.

Each state library has at a minimum a good selection of that state's records – vital statistics, copies (microfilms) of the US Censuses for that state, etc. See Appendix B for a listing of state libraries.

County Libraries

If you have the opportunity to visit the county library for the place where your ancestor(s) lived, you are most likely in for a treat. Some of my most pleasant genealogical memories are associated with prowling through county libraries. As with state libraries, county libraries are constrained by the budgeting that they have received. But I have found some wonderful nuggets in the county libraries I have done research in through the years.

Often, these libraries contain books of biographies that list the *Who's Who* of the counties – early pioneers, politicians, philanthropists, civil servants, etc. While your ancestors may not have been one of the founding fathers of the country, they may have played an important role in the early days of their county's development. You may also find old county newspapers, indexed obituaries, deed books, maps, wills, etc. that will assist you in your search for your ancestors.

One county library deserves special attention here. The Allen County Library in Fort Wayne, Indiana has been obsessed with maintaining and expanding its outstanding genealogical collection. Their collection is considered one of the most exceptional in the nation.

POIGNANT DISCOVERY

I knew that my 3rd great grandfather had served as a Colonel in the Civil War under Ulysses S. Grant, and I also knew that he was killed in a skirmish just prior to the Siege of Vicksburg. But I was unprepared for the article I found in his hometown newspaper:

Colonel Horney Killed!

"A private letter written to a gentleman in St. Louis, Missouri from Vicksburg under the date May 20th, and published in Monday morning's Democrat, gives the sad news that Colonel Leonidas Horney, of the 10th Missouri Regiment, was killed before Vicksburg. This is indeed bitter news to his family and many friends in this county. Let us hope the intelligence may not be confirmed."

Unfortunately, the intelligence was indeed confirmed. As an officer in the Civil War, the death of this small-town war hero had been an important event in the history of this town.

The Allen County Library set the standard for the genealogical world by developing an exhaustive index of genealogical articles that have been published in periodicals since 1847. The index covers subjects, surnames and locations. Called *PERSI* (*PER*iodical *S*ource *I*ndex), it is a wonderful tool.

The Allen County Library has launched a website that might be of interest to you: www.acpl.lib.in.us/genealogy/genealogy.html. Check it out - you just might find something that will assist you in finding that latest elusive ancestor you are seeking.

Genealogical and Historical Society Libraries

Many genealogical societies and state historical societies have collections of books, maps, deeds, and other materials that may be available for you to research. Often, those collections center on the surname and major branches off that surname that the genealogical organization is dedicated to researching. These societies often go to great lengths to locate and purchase books that contain information about the family. They may have also published books on your ancestors.

Some genealogical and historical societies lend their books out – in other words, they allow them to be taken from the premises just like a regular library. Others participate in the inter-library loan process, wherein individuals can request a book or microfilm from a library in another location and have it shipped to their local library. If you are planning a trip to a distant library, check to see if the book you are hoping to review is there before you go (it may be loaned out); a phone call to the library should answer the question.

University Libraries

All universities and colleges have libraries, and many of them have genealogy collections. Don't pass these up without a look. They are often the source of valuable genealogical information. I have spent many enjoyable and profitable hours in university libraries scouting for clues about my ancestors.

National Archives

There are fourteen locations of the National Archives geographically dispersed around the United States. Each contains a treasure trove of genealogical information, including all the US Censuses that are available for the public to view. Following are their locations:

Alaska
654 West Third Avenue
Anchorage, Alaska 99501-2145
Tel. 907/271-2441
E-mail: alaska.archives@nara.gov
Website: www.archives.gov/facilities/ak/anchorage.html

California
24000 Avila Road,
1st Floor, East Entrance
Laguna Niguel, California 92677-3497
Tel. 949/360-2641
E-mail: laguna.archives@nara.gov
Website: www.archives.gov/facilities/ca/laguna_niguel.html

1000 Commodore Drive
San Bruno, California 94066-2350
Tel. 650/876-9009
E-mail: sanbruno.archives@nara.gov
Website: www.archives.gov/facilities/ca/san_francisco.html

Colorado
Bldg. 48, Denver Federal Center
West 6th Avenue and Kipling Street
Denver, Colorado 80225-0307
Tel. 303/236-0806
E-mail: denver.archives@nara.gov
Website: www.archives.gov/facilities/co/denver.html

Georgia
1557 St. Joseph Avenue
East Point, Georgia 30344-2593
Tel. 404/763-7474
E-mail: atlanta.center@nara.gov
Website: www.archives.gov/facilities/ga/atlanta.html

Illinois
7358 South Pulaski Road
Chicago, Illinois 60629-5898
Tel. 773/581-7816
E-mail: chicago.archives@nara.gov
Website: www.archives.gov/facilities/il/chicago.html

Massachusetts
Frederick C. Murphy Federal Center
380 Trapelo Road
Waltham, Massachusetts 02452-6399
Tel. 781/647-8104
Tel. 866/406-2379

E-mail: waltham.center@nara.gov
Website: www.archives.gov/facilities/ma/boston.html

10 Conte Drive
Pittsfield, Massachusetts 01201-8230
Tel. 413/445-6885
E-mail: archives@pittsfield.nara.gov
Website: www.archives.gov/facilities/ma/pittsfield.html

Missouri
2312 East Bannister Road
Kansas City, Missouri 64131-3011
Tel. 816/926-6920
E-mail: kansascity.archives@nara.gov
Website: www.archives.gov/facilities/mo/kansas_city.html

New York
201 Varick Street
New York, New York 10014-4811
Tel. 212/337-1300
E-mail: newyork.archives@nara.gov
Website: www.archives.gov/facilities/ny/new_york_city.html

Pennsylvania
900 Market Street
Philadelphia, Pennsylvania 19107-4292
Tel. 215/597-3000
E-mail: philadelphia.archives@nara.gov
Website: www.archives.gov/facilities/pa/philadelphia_center_city.html

Texas
501 West Felix Street, Building 1
Fort Worth, Texas 76115-3405
Tel. 817/334-5525, ext. 243
E-mail: ftworth.archives@nara.gov
Website: www.archives.gov/facilities/tx/fort_worth.html

Washington
6125 Sand Point Way NE
Seattle, Washington 98115-7999
Tel. 206/526-6501
E-mail: seattle.archives@nara.gov
Website: www.archives.gov/facilities/wa/seattle.html

Washington DC
National Archives Building
700 Pennsylvania Avenue, N.W.
Washington DC
Tel. 866/272-6272
Website: www.archives.gov/

Hours vary from center to center. Generally, all offices are open Monday through Friday during normal business hours. Most offer at least one evening a week when they are open until 8:00pm and most are also open at least one if not two Saturdays per month.

The Hunt Begins!

So you have located a library that has a genealogical section, and you are hoping to find out something about an ancestor or two. What kinds of records might you find, and what kind of information can you hope to glean from those records? Following are a few of the more common types of records you may find. Remember that many of these records may be secondary resources of information, as the information may have been recorded years after an event occurred.

Vital Statistics Records

Many libraries have compendiums of information about births, deaths and marriages that took place within their city, county and/or state. Many times, local genealogical societies have gone to local government offices and gleaned and indexed information about these important genealogical events.

Census Records

Every state library and many county and local libraries have copies of the federal censuses that were conducted for their community. The state library will have copies of the census for the state, and city and county libraries may have them for the entire state or maybe just for the city or county they serve. A phone call to the library before going allows you to find out just what they have available in this area. See Chapter 11 for more on census research.

In addition to the US Census, many local censuses may have been taken that will shed light on your ancestors. Population, agricultural and other censuses may have been taken through the years in the community where your ancestor lived.

Biographies

I have had great success in finding biographies of several ancestors. Sometimes they are listed in *Who's Who* books of the city, county or state where they lived. I am not descended from royalty (few of us are), but at least a few of my ancestors played important roles in their communities, such as county surveyors, justices of the peace, businessmen, teachers, etc. Perhaps some of your ancestors did the same. Look for biographies, county and state histories. Most of these books have indexes or tables of contents that will allow you to quickly ascertain whether one of your ancestors is included.

Obituaries

Many library genealogy sections keep records of printed obituaries for the inhabitants of the community they serve. Some of these are kept alphabetically, some chronologically and indexed, or a combination of both. Obituaries are rich sources of clues. Following are information tidbits I have gleaned from obituaries through the years:

- Death date and place
- Burial date and place
- Birth date and place
- Names of parents
- Names of spouse and children
- Married names of daughters
- Places of residence of parents
- Places of residence of grown children
- Names of siblings
- Names of grandparents, aunts and uncles
- Address at time of death
- Occupation
- When they moved to the town/county/state
- Where they moved from
- Military service

When searching for obituaries, be creative. If the library doesn't have an indexed book of obituaries, do they have microfilms of old newspapers? If you know the approximate year of death, you can scan the obituary sections of weekly newspapers for several years pretty quickly. Several years ago I was looking for the obituary of a great uncle who lived in southern Colorado. I found out what newspapers were published in his small community (actually – in a small community nearby) and began searching.

I realized very quickly that the first newspaper of each year carried a list of all the deaths of county residents the previous year, along with their date of death. That allowed me to home in very quickly on the specific weekly edition I needed to search. I was able to find a ton of previously unknown genealogical information not only on him, but about his parents and several uncles. These clues allowed me to find more information about each of these individuals at a later date.

If you copy the information in an obituary, or even if you obtain a copy of the obituary, be sure and include the date the obituary appeared, and the name of the newspaper.

As a record of death, obituaries can be considered a primary genealogical source; as far as birth information it may contain, it is a secondary source.

Old Newspapers

Old newspapers from the community where your ancestors lived can provide a rich source of information and clues about your ancestors. As mentioned earlier, obituaries are found there, as well as human interest stories, classified ads, old advertisements, and interesting articles about the history of our country, especially during the time of presidential elections and wartime. These give you a flavor for what your ancestors were experiencing. And perhaps you'll discover the profession of your ancestor in an advertisement or an article about him or her.

Other information that might be found in a local newspaper includes:

• Obituaries
• Birth announcements
• Engagement or wedding announcements
• Visiting family members (out-of-town visitors were big news for local newspapers to report!)
• Notices of estate sales
• Property sales
• Letters to the editor
• Records of religious events: weddings, christenings, Bar or Bat Mitzvahs, etc.

Land Records

Many libraries contain records of land deals, surveys, deeds issued, etc. This information may not tell you an ancestor's birth date, but it may confirm that he or she lived in this community. It may also provide clues to aunts, uncles, grandparents, etc. that were living nearby. Often, I have found that land traded hands between family members.

City Telephone Directories

I have used city directories to help confirm the existence of an ancestor in that community at a certain time. I have also used it as a clue to indicate when an ancestor died or moved from the area. Once I found an obituary listing that mentioned a 2nd great uncle of mine – before that, I had no idea that he had lived in the area. The obituary indicated that this great uncle, who had been a relative of the deceased, had moved to the Portland area. I was able to use old city telephone directories to find out when he arrived in the area, and I learned when he left. That gave me an approximate year to begin searching in Portland for clues about this individual's arrival. A subsequent search enabled me to locate the individual in Portland.

Some city directories include a householders index, which listed the addresses that people were living at. This allowed me to locate individuals who were living with my relatives. In one case, it was a mother-in-law, in another it was a daughter and son-in-law of my ancestor.

Histories

Many libraries have histories – community as well as biographical – of the communities where they are located. These books can provide information about early settlers and prominent citizens. Keep an eye out: many of these books contain photos of the individuals whose biographies are contained therein. This may be the first glimpse of what the ancestor you are searching for looked like. For earlier generations, before photography was generally available, you may find a drawing of the individual.

Again – recognize that these books are secondary sources of information – to be used for clues to help you find primary sources.

Cemetery Indexes

Many genealogical libraries contain indexes for all the cemeteries in the communities they serve. These can be valuable, as they will help you identify where you might go to look at and take pictures of tombstones. Often, the books will give you the exact location of a tombstone.

Befriend the Librarian!

Spend a few minutes and get to know the librarian that is familiar with the genealogy section of the library you go to. Then don't be afraid to ask him or her about your search. If you explain what you're looking for, he or she may have suggestions about special collections the library has, or expedited ways to find what you are looking for. They will know whether special censuses were taken that might yield a clue to your ancestors, or whether certain records are available at the library to assist you in your search.

Collections & Libraries Checklist

Before going to the library in search of your ancestors, do or bring the following:

___ Determine who you are looking for.

___ What information do you want to find? Be open to other information you may run across.

___ Bring all the information you have about the person you are seeking: approximate birth dates and place, parents' names, etc.

___ Materials to record information: pens or pencils, pad of paper, family group sheets, etc.

___ Record the date you were in the library.

___ Record the name and address of the library you visited.

___ Record the information sources you searched through (it may be years until you return; no sense going through records you already searched!)

___ Record any information you find completely and accurately, including information about the source that provided the information.

___ Make copies of articles or microfilm pages that contain genealogical information.

___ Engage the librarian in your search; he or she may know of resources you hadn't thought of.

___ Be curious! Snoop through information sources that might contain additional information.

Additional Resources

Greenwood, Val D., *The Researcher's Guide to American Genealogy*, Genealogical Publishing Company, 2nd edition (April 1990)

Luebking, Sandra H. (Editor) and Eichholz, Alice, *The Source: A Guide of American Genealogy*, Ancestry Publishing (May 1997)

Mills, Elizabeth Shown, *Evidence! : Citation & Analysis for the Family Historian,* Genealogical Publishing Company (January 2000)

Guide to Genealogical Research in the National Archives, Church of Jesus Christ of Latter-day Saints.

9. Computers & the Internet

It's safe to say that the computer and the Internet are the two greatest aids to genealogical research to date.

While computers have been a boon to the business world, they have also opened up wide avenues for genealogists. Computer software has been designed to assist genealogists in keeping track of the legions of ancestors that they have searched out and identified, providing handy and efficient ways of grouping them into families and then displaying them, either on the screen or on paper.

The advent and proliferation of e-mail has also been a remarkable aid to genealogists. Communication about families that once took weeks or months now often takes moments, as information is often requested and exchanged in a matter of minutes. I have personally benefited from the use of e-mail in my genealogical research, as I have made and kept contact with individuals who are working on several of my lines.

The Internet

As wonderful as the computer is for organizing ancestral files and facilitating communication with others working on your family lines, perhaps its greatest value is in providing a gateway to the Internet. The Internet is a powerful tool that enables genealogists to research records located literally anywhere in the world. Formerly, many of these records were virtually unavailable to genealogists simply because of the expense that would have been incurred in traveling to distant locations to view the records. But that is no longer the case. Many of those records are available on-line, and are only a mouse click or two away from researchers.

To illustrate the power I speak of, try this experiment: Go to the Internet, and using whichever search engine you are most familiar with (Yahoo!, Lycos, AltaVista, Excite, Hotbot, Infoseek, etc.), type in your last name (or the last name of an ancestor) and the word *genealogy*, and click on *Search*. I did this for a number of my lines, and here are the number of hits I came up with for each (a "hit" is Internet lingo for "how many websites were found with the information you requested"):

• Cunningham – 8
• Horney – 32
• Hudson – 12
• Lowrance – 1,070
• McCollough – 401
• Phillips – 13
• Quillen – 1
• Ritchey – 4,100
• Sellers – 2
• Stunkard – 50
• Throckmorton – 2
• Turpin – 1

Each one of these hits has the potential of yielding information about a family member for whom you have been searching in vain. And more often than not, the information doesn't stop there – my experience is that once I find one person in this manner, there are often two, three or more generations beyond that included in the listing.

Genealogy Websites

There are literally tens of thousands, perhaps hundreds of thousands of websites devoted to genealogical research, all just a mouse click away. The Internet is the largest genealogy library in the world. Listed below are some of my favorite and most productive websites, and a little about each of them.

Cyndi's List of Genealogy Sites on the Internet (www.cyndislist.com). When you think of Cyndi's List, you should think of a mammoth card catalog in the sky - it is a gigantic index of genealogical websites. When you go to Cyndi's List, one of the first things you see will be the number of active links available through Cyndi's List. It seems that every time I log onto Cyndi's List, the number of websites grows. At the time of this writing, the number of links is 152,050! Now that's a lot of websites.

In addition to being an index, Cyndi's List provides links to each website listed, so once you find a website that catches your interest, you merely click on the link and you are there. It is remarkably user friendly, and is a great place to begin your on-line research. If there is a weakness on Cyndi's List, it is the many, many website links that are there. You'll be like a kid in a candy store, bedazzled and unsure where to turn next.

Earlier in this chapter I suggested you enter the word *genealogy* along with your surname, or the surname for one of your ancestors, into a search engine and see how many hits you could get. I entered the same surnames again on Cyndi's List, and here are the number of hits I got for each name:

	Yahoo!	Cyndi's List
Cunningham	8	2,750
Horney	32	68
Hudson	12	3,373
Lowrance	1,070	116
McCollough	401	216
Phillips	13	6,182
Quillen	1	161
Ritchey	4,100	1,524
Sellers	2	1,384
Stunkard	50	12
Throckmorton	2	287
Turpin	1	601

(Note: To get to these Cyndi's List pages, I entered *Personal Home Pages* in the box on the home page of Cyndi's list. Then I selected any of the personal home pages that were displayed. At the bottom left-hand side of each personal home page is an alphabet for you to begin spelling the surnames you are looking for.)

Some of these hits are websites containing information about each surname. Others are links to message boards where people leave information about individuals, or leave queries about individuals ("Can anyone provide me information about my 2nd great grandfather Jonathan Baldwin Quillen? I think he was born in..."), and a host of other sites of genealogical value.

I guarantee that you will find something of genealogical interest if you visit Cyndi's List. As you learn to work with it and navigate around, you will be amazed at the wide variety of resources that are available there. Below are just a few of the many categories that are available on Cyndi's List:

- **African American** – tools to assist you in doing genealogical research for African American ancestors.
- **Austria** – If your ancestors came from Austria, here is good place to begin your search for them.
- **Births and Baptisms** – lists of vital records (birth, marriage, death) for a number of states.
- **Catholic** – links to many Catholic genealogical sources. The Catholic Church has been a prolific recorder of important and vital genealogical information for centuries.

- **Eastern Europe** – So your ancestors came from countries formerly behind the Iron Curtain? Don't despair – there are dozens of links that will help you begin or enhance your search.
- **Death Records** – Have you had any ancestors die? Many of them may be waiting to be found in the nearly 500 death record links available here.
- **Handwriting and Script** – several dozen links to resources that will help you decipher those sometimes-unintelligible scribbles on genealogical records.
- **Hispanic, Central and South America, and the West Indies** – there are over 400 links dealing with individuals from this part of the world.
- **How-To** – now that you have this book, you'll have less need for these sites, although you may glean a nugget or two.
- **Immigration and Naturalization** – here are over 300 sites that will help you find those intrepid ancestors who left all to come to America.
- **Jewish** – nearly 400 links that focus on your Jewish roots.
- **Military Resources Worldwide** – the military often kept detailed records of its members, including family relationships.
- **Native American** – over 300 links assist those researching their Native American roots.
- **Obituaries** – over 250 links that might help you find the obituary of some ancestor. Obituaries are often a rich source of genealogical information.
- **Prisons, Prisoners and Outlaws** – yes, most of us have a few horse thieves in our ancestry!
- **Professional Researchers, Volunteers and Other Research Services** – over 800 links that may provide possible options to help you clamber over genealogical stumbling blocks.
- **Surnames, Family Associations and Newsletters** – nearly 5,500 family and genealogical organizations that may help you with your research.
- **Western Europe** – if you are like most Americans, you'll benefit from the many links that will assist you in doing research in this region of the world.
- **Wills and Probate** – another rich source of genealogical information when all else has failed.

The above list barely scratches the surface of what you will find on Cyndi's List. I guarantee you will find Cyndi's List to be most helpful and intriguing.

Ellis Island website. If your ancestors came to America between 1892 and 1924, you'll definitely want to check out www.ellisisland.org, the official website for that immigration gateway into the United States. During that time, more than 12 million individuals were processed through her gates, all headed for the freedoms America offered.

Before you can do much on the website, you must register. This is a relatively painless (and free) process that takes all of one or two minutes. Once registered, you'll be able to tour around and see most of the information available on the website.

The most robust feature of the website is the *Passenger Search*, which allows you to search for your ancestor among the 22 million passengers whose names were on passenger lists (also called *ship manifests*) of ships that arrived at Ellis Island. These individuals may have been passengers, immigrants or crew members who arrived in America between 1892 and 1924. Volunteers spent years microfilming, transcribing, cataloging and indexing the information for the Ellis Island Foundation. And now the information is available to you.

Getting information from the website is quite easy. From the home page of ellisisland.org, click on *Passenger Search*, then click on *New Search* on the page that appears. On the next page, type the first and last names (at least the last name) of the ancestor you are looking for, indicate whether they are male or female, and then click on *Continue*.

Let's use an example. The original spelling of my surname was McQuillan, and my ancestors came to America from the area that is now Northern Ireland. If I enter the name McQuillan in the required box and click *Continue*, I learn that 335 people with the surname McQuillan were listed on passenger lists between 1892 and 1924. The first page lists the first 25 individuals that were found. The list includes the names of the passengers, their residence, the year they arrived, and their age on arrival. Since my family is from Northern Ireland, I scan the list looking for people whose residence is listed as being from Ireland. The first page tells me that a Philip McQuillan came to America from Belfast, Ireland (Northern Ireland did not exist as an entity until 1922) in 1915. Clicking on his name (which is linked to his passenger record), the following information appears:

Name: Philip McQuillan
Ethnicity: Britain
Place of Residence: Belfast, Ireland
Date of Arrival: October 31, 1915
Age on Arrival: 33 years
Gender: Male
Marital Status: Single
Ship of Travel: New York
Port of Departure: Liverpool, England

While this summary does not contain primary genealogical source information, it has a number of secondary information tidbits that might be of use to me as I search for more information about this possible ancestor. It tells me his place of residence was Belfast. It tells me he was 33 in 1915, which translates to an approximate birth date of 1881 or 1882. (Assuming he wasn't fibbing about his age, he would have been born in 1882 if his birthday was before October 31, or in 1881 if his birthday was between November 1 and December 31.) It tells me that he was single, and that he departed from Liverpool, England. That last tidbit is interesting. There were a number of Irish ports that transatlantic ships departed from (Queenstown / Cobh, Belfast, Derry), but he departed from Liverpool, England. That tells me that even though he considered his residence as Belfast, he may have been working in England (as many of his fellow countrymen did – and still do).

On the same page where this information is displayed, there are two nice options, especially if you know or believe this passenger is an ancestor. If you click on the button that says *View Original Ship Manifest*, you will be taken to a page with a photograph of the actual passenger list where your ancestor's name is written. The picture can be enlarged (look for the small icon of a magnifying glass), and a veritable genealogical treasure awaits you. The ship's manifest collected an amazing (and sometimes startling!) set of facts about the individual, including some wonderful genealogical clues. Many of the questions are similar to those found on the US Census. The ship manifest questions changed somewhat from year to year, but regardless of the year they provide interesting information on each passenger. In 1915, the questions asked (and answered) were:

- Were they a citizen, diplomat, tourist, or a citizen of Canada, China or Mexico?
- What was their age in years and months?
- What was their sex and marital status?
- What was their occupation, and could they read and write?
- What was their nationality and race?
- What was their last permanent address?
- What was the name and complete residence address of a relative or friend in the country from whence they came?
- What was the passenger's final destination (state and town)?
- Did they have a ticket to their final destination?
- Who paid the passage for this individual?
- Did they have at least $50? If not, how much did they have?
- Had they been to the United States before, and if so, where and for how long?
- Were they coming to visit a relative or friend? And if so, who was it and what was their full address?
- Were they a polygamist?
- Were they an Anarchist?
- What was their mental and physical health condition?
- Were they deformed or crippled, and if so, the nature, length of time and cause?

• Did they have any identifying marks?
• What was their height, complexion and color of hair and eyes?
• Where was their place of birth?

You can see why some of this information would make a genealogist's heart flutter! In the case of Philip McQuillan, in addition to what we learned on the summary page (his age, marital status, residence, and place of departure), we learn that he was:

• a dairyman;
• from Belfast;
• the son of William McQuillan of Fairview Glen Road in Belfast;
• going to see his brother, James McQuillan, who lived on Liberty Avenue in
    Pittsburgh, Pennsylvania;
• not a polygamist or anarchist (thank goodness!);
• had no "deformities" or identifying marks;
• 5'-3" with a light complexion, brown hair and blue eyes;
• born in Belfast.

Wow! What a wonderful (secondary) source of genealogical information. From the ship's manifest we learned the approximate year of his birth, the name of his father, the fact that he had a brother named James who lived in Pittsburgh, and that Philip was born in Belfast.

From this information, I have more information that will help me do research not only on James, but also for his father William and his brother James.

For a few dollars you can receive a copy of the original passenger list. An 11"x17" copy will cost you $25, and a 17"x22" copy will cost you $35. Caution: the ship's manifest was kept in large log books, and to get all the information, you would have to purchase both pages that the information extended over, so the entire cost would be double the above prices. But if this were truly an ancestor, what a prize to have a copy of!

Also available to view and/or purchase is a photograph of the ship that your ancestor came to America in. Back on the web page that listed the summary of the passenger's information is a label entitled *View Ship*. Just click on that label and *voila* – there is the picture of the ship. You may also purchase this picture for $10.00 or $12.50, depending on whether you want a 5"x7" or 9"x12" picture. Again, I think this would be a wonderful thing to have for an ancestor.

As you search for ancestors on the website, you are given the opportunity to save any searches that you are conducting, so you capture all the information as you go along. That way, if your research trips are hours, days or weeks (or months!) apart, you don't have to replow old ground.

The Ellis Island website also provides a nice opportunity to start a *Family Scrapbook*. Accessed via an icon on the Ellis Island home page, this section of the website allows you to create an on-line scrapbook for your ancestors. You may add stories, photos and other information about your ancestors and have it be included in the Ellis Island Family History Archive. To access this section and create your family scrapbook, you need to become a "sustaining member" of The Statue of Liberty-Ellis Island Foundation. A one-year membership costs $45.00. The membership fee enables the organization to continue to provide a number of great services to visitors to Ellis Island – those who come in person as well as those who are virtual visitors.

All immigrants who came to America came through Ellis Island, right? Wrong! Ellis Island was the busiest port of entry (and the one with the best PR agent?) but there were many other entry points into the US, including Baltimore, Detroit, New Orleans, Philadelphia, and San Francisco. This is certainly not an exhaustive list, so don't be discouraged if you don't find your ancestors on any of their passenger lists.

FamilyToolbox.net. FamilyToolbox.net is another of the major genealogy websites that serves as a card catalog (or *toolbox*, if you wish) of genealogy sites on the Internet. At the time of this writing, it did not have nearly as many sites as Cyndislist.com, but it organized itself in an entirely different manner. While I did not find it as intuitive as Cyndi's List, other researchers like it better.

It contains links to a variety of genealogical resources, such as bulletin boards, mailing lists, query boards, computer software for genealogy and other topics of interest to genealogists.

One of the features I like about FamilyToolbox.net is that throughout the website, there are many helpful links that provide advice on a wide variety of topics. These might be information about the latest edition of genealogy software that has come out, or new records that the government has made available, articles on a specific research topic, etc.

FamilyToolbox.net is sponsored by businesses that target genealogists. That sponsorship takes the form of frequent advertisements that pop up on the screen, and many of the screens have static advertisements on them. While these are sometimes helpful, I generally find them a bit blatant and annoying. Cindi's List also has a few advertisements, but they are not as intrusive as on this website. FamilyToolbox.net also can also be accessed via **www.genealogytoolbox.com**.

Random Acts of Genealogical Kindness – this is one of my favorite genealogy sites on the Internet! I think it symbolizes the values of genealogical generosity that most genealogists are known for. The website is **www.raofk.org**, and I guarantee you will find it to your liking.

The premise is this: thousands of genealogists offer their time and research talents to do research for other genealogists who live in other parts of the world. For example, a genealogist in Hemmingen, Germany might volunteer to do a variety of genealogy-related research projects for anyone needing that research. They might go check out a nearby cemetery, searching for specific surnames. Or they might go to the local magistrate's office to review a marriage log book, or a local parish to scan the birth and baptismal registry from 100 years ago. The organization asks its members to donate at least one search a month, for which they receive no pay. If you want someone to do some research for you, you need to volunteer to do at least one search for someone else. The only cost to the requesting genealogist is for specific costs related to the search: photocopying, gas (if the search is done far from the researcher), etc.

What a great site.

There are a number of genealogy sites that offer advanced research capabilities for those willing to pay a pretty healthy subscription fee. Two of the best known are **Genealogy.com** (www.genealogy.com) and **Ancestry.com** (www.ancestry.com). They are sites that offer subscribers a variety of databases through which they can comb in search of their ancestors. For example, as of this writing, Genealogy.com offers a $99.99 one-year subscription that provides access to their US Census database. Subscribers will be able to view images (photos) of actual census pages. If $99.99 seems a little steep for you, they also offer a monthly subscription for $19.99 per month, which can be canceled with 30 days notice. Genealogy.com's website also includes free online classes, articles and advice from professional genealogists, and an extensive collection of proprietary data.

Other services and databases are also available for a fee, as are a number of CD ROM collections.

As you use these services, be aware that most of the actual research information you would like has a price tag attached to it. There are very effective links and enticements that make you feel like you are going to get your answer, only to find that you are led down a path that ends in an offer to buy a subscription, CD or newsletter that might provide the information you are looking for.

AOL.com – Yes, that Master of E-mail also offers a pretty impressive genealogy website at hometown.aol.com/USgenealogy (note: no *www.* is required). From that home page, type in a search term such as *Irish Genealogy* or *Hispanic Genealogy* and click on *Search*. You'll be taken to a set of links that match your request – and the hunt is on! There are a wide variety of sites available – many of which are merely links to subscription services such as Genealogy.com and Ancestry.com.

Another area of the AOL-sponsored website that I really like is their Genealogy Forum website (www.genealogyforum.com) that is extremely helpful and quite easy to use. From the home page, click on any of several topics, and you'll be taken to a link that may be of use to you. For example, click on the *Messages* icon and you'll be taken to a message board where individuals post information about various individuals. Perhaps you'll find one of your ancestors hiding there. Under the same icon, look for *Ethnic Resources*, and you're given a choice of African American, Irish, Hispanic, Huguenot, Jewish and Native American links. Click on any of these, and you'll be whisked to a host of websites specializing in the ethnic research area you specified.

Genealogy Software

There are dozens of software packages available on the market today that will help you keep your genealogical research organized. While notebooks and file folders are fine to get you started, as you progress you'll want to begin saving and organizing your genealogy in a more readily accessible fashion, and genealogy software will help you do that. Genealogy software on the market today allows you to input critical information about your ancestors and then provides very simple ways to retrieve and display the information. Using the information you have input, it will gather your ancestors into families in a heartbeat, produce pedigree charts in the blink of an eye, and provide instant access to the 1,000s of records you may have about your ancestors.

As you begin your search for a software package that will work best for you, you'll be amazed (I am, anyway) by the many clever names of genealogy software programs out there: BirthWrite, Brother's Keeper, Family Ties, Family Treemaker, Family Matters and Relatively Yours, to name a few.

So what should you look for when you finally decide to organize all your manual and paper records into a software program? The first and foremost thing I think is important is user friendliness. No matter how powerful your genealogy program is, or how much storage space it has, if you don't understand how to use it, it is of no real use to you. From a capacity and capability standpoint, most of the major software programs available today are pretty much the same, especially for those who are just beginning their genealogical quest.

I have one caution: be certain that whichever program you choose, whether you are a beginner or not, is capable of **GEDCOM** capability. GEDCOM is an acronym for **GE**nealogical **D**ata **COM**munication. It allows you to share your data with other genealogists, and also allows it to be ported (transferred) to other genealogy programs. If you choose a software program that uses proprietary formatting, you will not be able to share or transfer information except to users who use the same program as you. Fortunately, GEDCOM is a pretty standard default for the software programs on the market today, but it is wise to check to make sure.

One other caution: Be sure and check the computer system requirements before you buy. Do you have the horsepower on your computer to run the program – do you even have the space on your hard drive to install it? Once you open the box, you bought it, and as with all software - no returns allowed!

It would be really nice if you could take the various genealogy software programs on the market for a "test drive" so that you can try it out before purchasing it. Fortunately, many of the more popular genealogy programs on the market today provide a demo version of their software that you can play with on their website.

Following are some of the more popular and capable genealogy programs out there:

Personal Ancestral File, more commonly known as PAF, is produced by the Church of Jesus Christ of Latter-day Saints. The LDS Church pioneered the use of software for storing and retrieving genealogy data with several early DOS versions of PAF.

Now all grown up, the Windows version of PAF is one of the most widely used genealogy software programs today. Although it does not provide as many life events as some other programs, it collects the basic and most critical information: birth, baptism, marriage, death and burial dates for each individual. In addition, each event allows you to enter notes regarding the source of information, or just about anything you would like to add.

This is the software program I currently use. I find it intuitive (that is – I can figure it out myself without having to read the manuals) and it has plenty of storage capability for me.

PAF is considered the Ford or Chevy of genealogy software programs: while it is not as flashy or elegant as some other models, it provides good, reliable service.

PAF has a nice array of reports and charts available. It can produce, either on screen or on paper, family histories, pedigree charts, family group records, and other reports. It will convert data from former versions of PAF software, so presumably, as new versions of the software are produced the ability to convert the last version of PAF software will be available. PAF allows you to attach a person's picture with their record. It also has the ability to generate HTML Web pages.

There is no demo version of the software available. However, there is no need: PAF is available for free from the LDS Church simply by going to their family history website, www.familysearch.org.™ If you cannot download the software from the Internet, you may also order CD or diskette versions of PAF from their website for as little as $6.00, or by calling the Distribution Center (Tel. 800/537-5950).

A lot of the popularity of PAF derives from its price (free) and the fact that it has TempleReady capabilities, a feature that allows LDS genealogists to prepare their records for temple work.

Family Origins is another popular genealogy software program on the market today. It is available from FormalSoft, Inc. (PO Box 495, Springville, Utah 84663). While PAF might be classed as a Ford or a Chevy, Family Origins is probably more in the Cadillac or BMW class because if its extra features. For example, where PAF allows you to identify the basic facts about each person (name, birth, death, marriage, etc.), Family Origins provides over 50 pre-identified information events, including occupation, religion, graduation dates, divorce, etc. If the need strikes you, you can also create your own information categories. It is also one of the few other programs on the market today that provides TempleReady capabilities for its LDS users. This feature alone guarantees it a significant number of additional sales.

Of all the features Family Origins has, the one that most impresses me is its intuitive and user-friendly interface. Some programs on the market just seem too difficult to use. True, they may have great power, but they also require you (or so it seems) to be a computer programmer to get the most out of them. That isn't the case with Family Origins. Even if this is your first venture into a software program, you should find it relatively easy to use. Yet it also has all the horsepower necessary for really advanced genealogists – a great combination.

Family Origins includes a number of nice printing capabilities, including a broad set of reports and family trees. It also includes the capability to create a multimedia scrapbook by allowing you to attach photographs, sound clips, and video clips to any person, family, place, source, or event. It also has the ability to generate HTML web pages.

While PAF is my sentimental favorite, Family Origins has the horsepower to do some really fun things with your genealogy. (It even has a family reunion organizer with all sorts of tips and planning assists.)

The Family Origins website is www.formalsoft.com, and you can download a working copy of Family Origins from their website. You may keep it for a 15-day free trial. You may order your copy of Family Origins by calling 866/GENEALOGY (866/436-3256). At the time of publication, the cost was $29.95 for the latest version.

Family Treemaker is another of the powerful, popular genealogy software packages on the market. With packages ranging from $49.99 to $99.99, it is a little more expensive than some of the other high-performing packages available. Family Treemaker is available at many retail outlets as well as from its manufacturer, Broderbund LLC (www.broderbund.com).

A rich feature set includes well-regarded charts and a strong website generation capability. You can post some of the charts that are available on the Genealogy.com website for free, thus allowing you to share your findings with others. As with the other software programs reviewed here, Family Treemaker has the reputation of being easy to use and easy to navigate in.

Various packages are offered, with the more expensive packages coming with packs of CDs that contain valuable historical data covering over 1,100 years.

There are several features I like in Family Treemaker. First of all, it has an e-mail storage capability that allows you to store the e-mail addresses of other researchers you are communicating with. Gone are the "yellow stickies" with names and e-mail addresses that plague my desktop. I also like the date calculator that allows me to determine the day of the week for any given date in any given year.

The photo capability is great in Family Treemaker, allowing you to create electronic scrapbooks and then print directly from those scrapbooks. Photos can also be linked to specific ancestors, and source materials (birth, death and marriage certificates, wills, etc.) can be scanned and then linked to a specific event.

Earlier versions of **Ancestral Quest** were once regarded as the Number 1 genealogy software on the market. Other software manufacturers have since put their development efforts in high gear and have caught and in some cases surpassed their capabilities. But they are still a strong competitor, worthy of your consideration. Ancestral Quest was developed by Incline Software (PO Box 95543, South Jordan, UT 84095-0543, 800/825-8864 or 801/280-4434). It is available from some retail outlets as well as several websites, including www.softwareoasis.net/dvdz.htm and Ancestral Quest's website at www.ancquest.com. The cost at the time of publication is $37.95.

The documentation that accompanies the product is some of the best on the market, and for those who rely heavily on documentation to learn or feel comfortable with a software product, this is a real selling point. It is relatively easy to use software, especially for basic data entry, printing, etc. But for the more advanced features, the documentation is a huge plus.

Ancestral Quest allows you to attach photos, audio and video clips to individuals in such a manner that allow you to create a memorable multimedia keepsake scrapbook. It also has more than adequate report and charting capabilities, including the production of large (320 inch by 320 inch) wall charts.

One feature that excites many genealogists is Ancestral Quest's PAF compatibility. PAF 3.0 and 4.0 records can be read and edited without importing or conversion. And why not? Software developers from Incline Software (the developers of Ancestral Quest) assisted the LDS Church in their development of PAF. Ancestral Quest 4.0 and later versions can also read PAF 5.0 and later files, but cannot edit them. But what do you do if you need the files edited? Simple – since PAF is free, just download the latest version, edit the required files in PAF, and then move them over to Ancestral Quest! They are also one of the few programs on the market today that has TempleReady capability for LDS users.

Ancestral Quest's marketing materials say, "(Ancestral Quest's) format is perfect for the beginner and yet powerful enough for the most advanced genealogist." And I have to agree that it is more than merely marketing hype – they do seem to have been successful in blending ease of use with great power.

Ultimate Family Tree is another of the powerful, popular and user-friendly genealogy programs on the market. Developed and marketed by The Learning Company (88 Rowland Way, Novatao, California 94945. Tel. 415/895-2000), it is considered a very well-rounded software package, garnering high marks from users for its charts, reports and publishing capabilities. It is available from many retail outlets as well as from their website at www.uftree.com.

Ultimate Family Tree offers unlimited personal events (birth, marriage, death, occupation, religion, military service, etc.) for genealogists to use. But its claim to fame is a variety of source citation templates that provide users with easy-to-use templates for the most common source documents.

In what has become a fairly standard feature for most genealogy programs, Ultimate Family Tree provides you with the capability to create and launch your own genealogy web page, including scanned photos, audio and video clips, etc.

Sound interesting? Go ahead – take it for a spin before you buy - you may download a free demo version of the software from their website.

Can you stand one more genealogy software review? Another of the powerful yet affordable genealogy software programs on the market is **Legacy**. It comes standard with many of the features its competitors have, but this software is exceptionally intuitive. I particularly like the way it lays out its various pages – they are easy to read and presented in a manner that are visually appealing and that make sense to me. Legacy allows you to enter millions of names (provided you have the disk space), with multiple events for each person. Add photographs, sound bytes or video clips and you've got a great repository for your family records. Add to that its Internet and web page creation capabilities, along with the ability to print a family book complete with pictures and you have a versatile, powerful software package.

The standard edition is $19.95, and the deluxe edition is $29.95. While there are a few additional features available in the deluxe edition, the main difference is that the standard edition is downloaded from the legacy website (www.legacyfamilytree.com) and the deluxe edition provides its software on CD and provides a User's Guide.

Computer & Internet Checklist

___ Does your computer have Internet capability?

___ Do you have an Internet Service Provider? If not, determine which one best meets your needs and budget.

___ Determine the ancestor or surname you want to research.

___ Do you have any clues about your ancestor that might enable you to find them?
>___ County, state or country of birth
>• Country of immigration?
>• Approximate date of immigration?
>___ Did he serve in the military?
>___ Etc.

___ Select a software package that meets your needs. (Make sure your computer has the memory, horsepower and right operating system to run it!)

___ Decide whether you want to subscribe to one of the genealogy subscription services (Genealogy.com, Ancestry.com, etc.).

Additional Resources

Colletta, John Philip, *They Came in Ships: A Guide to Finding Your Immigrant Ancestor's Ship*, Ancestry Publishing. (March 1998)

Howells, Cyndi, *Netting Your Ancestors: Genealogical Research on the Internet,* Genealogical Publishing Company. (1999)

McClure, Rhonda, *The Complete Idiot's Guide to Online Genealogy*, Alpha Books, 2nd edition. (January 2002)

Tepper, Michael, *American Passenger Arrival Records — A Guide to the Records of Immigrants,* Genealogical Publishing Company. (1999)

10. Using the LDS Church

The Genealogical Societyof Utah, affiliated with the Church of Jesus Christ of Latter-day Saints, is one of the premier genealogical organizations in the world. The Genealogical Societyof Utah and the **LDS church** have been actively involved in collecting genealogical information for over 150 years. Working with foreign governments, they have been methodically and tirelessly microfilming countless governmental and church records throughout the world. Even as you read this, hundreds of volunteers are scattered across the globe microfilming records. At the time of this printing, records have been filmed in over 110 countries.

The good news is that this information is then archived, and is available to anyone with a willingness to search through their records for them - whether they are members of the LDS church or not. There are three important areas you need to learn about as you become familiar with this wonderful resource for research. Those three areas are:

• Family History Library
• Family History Centers
• FamilySearch™ website

Let's talk about each one of these resources:

The Family History Library
Nerve central for all this genealogical activity is in Salt Lake City, Utah in a large building known as the **Family History Library**. The library was founded in 1894 with the intent of assisting members of the LDS church with their family history research. Since that time, the library and its resources have been made available to all, regardless of their religious affiliation. The building that currently houses the library was built in 1985, and is located at 35 North West Temple in Salt Lake City (Tel. 801/240-2331). It is open Monday from

7:30am to 5:00pm, and Tuesday through Saturday from 7:30am to 10:00pm. It is closed on Sundays, January 1, July 4, Thanksgiving and December 24 and 25.

The genealogical collection is housed on five floors (four of them open to the public). At 142,000 square feet, it is the largest library of its kind in existence. Lighting, humidity and temperature control in the library are designed to protect the precious genealogical records from deterioration.

And is it ever a busy place! Hundreds of volunteers and full- and part-time employees labor to assist an average of 2,000 visitors that come through its doors each day. There is no charge to enter the library or use its services, nor is there a need to call for reservations.

The library boasts a genealogical collection that makes the mouth of any genealogist water. It has over 2.2 million rolls of microfilmed genealogical records, and 742,000 microfiche. There are over 300,000 books in the library's collections, most of them family histories. Their genealogical collection grows - mostly through the efforts of volunteers – at the rate of nearly 50,000 rolls of microfilm annually. It is estimated that over *750 million* names are contained in these records. That's a lot of people, and many of your ancestors are likely to be contained in those records.

Genealogical records are available from the United States, Canada, Europe, the British Isles, Latin America, Asia and Africa. The vast majority of the collection contains information on individuals that died prior to 1920.

I have been to the Family History Library, and it is as impressive as it sounds. For a time, I was fortunate enough to live in Salt Lake City, and I worked just a few blocks from the Library. Often, I would arrange to take my morning break at 11:45am, my lunch at noon and my afternoon break at 1:00pm, giving me nearly an hour and a half to do research on a fairly regular basis. Good idea, right? Wrong...I had to stop that practice because I found that I was continually calling back to work and taking the afternoon off as vacation because I had found a lead I just had to follow up on. While my ancestors loved it, my wife was not too thrilled about the practice.

Volunteers and employees in the Family History Library are anxious to assist you in your research efforts, whether you are just beginning your search, or whether you have been doing it for many years. They have experts in a variety of areas, including various foreign countries. They can help you get started or continue to unravel a genealogical mystery that you have been wrestling with for years.

Once you arrive, you'll find a host of supporting resources available to you in addition to the vast genealogical collection. There are over 500 microfilm and microfiche readers, over 160 computers available for visitors' use, copy machines for books and for microfilm. There are even scanners available that allow you to transfer information you find on microfilm to a CD. Tables and chairs are spread throughout the facility to allow you to study various and sundry materials.

The Library regularly schedules a variety of classes, including orientation classes and classes that focus on specialized research techniques. Call ahead or visit www.familysearch.org to see when these classes are scheduled.

It is impossible to have all these genealogical records stored on-site. Although most are there, and many are available via computer, it is wise to contact the Family History Library about four weeks before you visit to arrange for records that might not be kept on-site. To learn what records are available before your visit, go to **www.familysearch.org** and select *Library* and then click on *Family History Library Catalog*.

I have had personal experiences of finding long lost relatives while researching within the walls of this Library, and many friends can tell stories of searches with happy endings as a result of visits to the Family History Library.

Getting Around Salt Lake City

If you are fortunate enough to travel to Salt Lake City to visit and spend time in the Family History Library, you will likely be befuddled by seemingly incomprehensible addresses in Salt Lake City. You'll encounter addresses like:

709 North 700 East
2392 East 4400 South
1332 West 7100 South

Confusing, right? Wrong - once you understand the format, you will never need a map to get around in Salt Lake City. And the format is logical and easy: the first number and direction represent the street address; the second number and direction are the name of the street. There – got it? No? Read on.

The key to unfolding the mystery of these addresses is the LDS Temple in downtown Salt Lake City. All addresses in Salt Lake City tell you their relative location to the temple. For example, the address 4684 West 3100 South tells you that the house or building is located 46.84 blocks west of the temple and is on 3100 South Street (which is 31 blocks south of the temple). Taking the addresses above, the first is 7.09 blocks north of the temple and is on 700 East Street; the next is 23.92 blocks east of the temple on 4400 South Street, and the last is 13.32 blocks west of the temple on 7100 South Street (which is 71 blocks south of the temple).

The addresses immediately around the temple have a slightly more conventional naming scheme, but they still center on the temple. For example, the address of the Family History Library is 35 North West Temple. That tells you that the Library is .35 blocks north of the temple, and on West Temple Street. West Temple Street is the street that runs along the west side of the temple – also known as 100 West.

Once you understand the format, you will never need a map when looking for an address in Salt Lake City (or in most Utah towns, for that matter). In recent years it has been fashionable to name streets more conventional names, like Cherry Lane, Elm Street, etc. When faced with an incomprehensible address like 3145 South Maple Avenue, simply ask for the numbered street name of Maple Avenue, and you'll be told something like 2950 West. So now you know that the address on Maple Avenue is 31.45 blocks south of the temple on 2950 West Street.

Family History Centers

Okay, so you don't live in the Rocky Mountain region of the United States, nor do you plan on going to Utah any time soon. Does that mean that you are out of luck, that all these fabulous records are simply tantalizingly outside your grasp? Fortunately for you and me, the answer is, "Of course not." The LDS Church has provided alternate access to all of their genealogical records via their **Family History Centers**.

Considered branches to the Family History Library in Salt Lake City, Family History Centers are located literally throughout the world. Each is staffed by local volunteers who are interested in helping you conduct research on your family.

As of this printing, there are over 3,700 Family History Centers spread throughout the world, operating in every state in the United States and in nearly 100 countries throughout the world. And they are heavily used – over 100,000 rolls of microfilm are circulated to Family History Centers *monthly* – over one million rolls per year!

To determine whether there are any Family History Centers near you (there almost certainly are), go to the LDS Church's website at www.familysearch.org. Click on the *Family History Centers* label and you will be directed to a page where you can enter the city and state or country where you live, and within seconds you will be advised of any Family History Centers near you.

The hours of operation at the Family History Centers vary from center to center. Since each center is staffed solely by volunteers, the hours are dependent on the volunteers' availability. Generally speaking, each FHC is open two or three days a week for anywhere from four to twelve hours on those days. The telephone numbers listed are generally for phones located within the Center; if you get no answer to your call, try at various times, especially in the evenings between 6:00pm and 9:00pm. Or you can merely stop by the address and if the center is not open, there is almost always a sign indicating the hours the Family History Center is open. To narrow your time search, it is important to know that Family History Centers are never open on Sundays or Mondays. If you do not have Internet access, call 800/346-6044 and representatives there will help identify the closest Family History Center to you.

Many of the records that are housed at the Family History Library are available to researchers at each Family History Center. If you identify a record you want to search, you may order it through your local Family History Center. For a small postage fee (as of this writing: $3.25 for microfilm and $.15 per microfiche page), you can order most of these records. Microfilm or microfiche will arrive within a week or two (usually) at your local Family History Center, and you will be notified of their arrival. You may then go to the Center to view the microfilm or microfiche. They will remain in your local Center for six weeks, giving you ample time to review them. If for some reason that is not enough time, then you can extend them for another six weeks.

Each Family History Center is also equipped with computers and Internet access so that you can access the many records available on CD as well as contact the LDS Church's genealogy website, www.familysearch.org.

Getting the Most Out of Your Local Family History Center

As wonderful as they are, Family History Centers will be much more useful if you follow some basic guidelines.

Prepare

Before you go to your local Family History Center, prepare for your visit. Have an idea about what line of your family (or what individual) you want to search for. Gather all the information you possibly can about the person or line that you want to research. Know surnames, city, county and/or state where they lived, and approximate dates of birth. The more information you can bring with you, the higher your likelihood of succeeding in your search.

Call Ahead

Before you just show up at one of the Family History Centers near you, call the contact number and confirm the location and hours of operation. Because the Centers are staffed solely by volunteers, Center hours and days of operation may vary as volunteers come and go. The website might not have the latest information on hours of operation.

If you are not successful in reaching anyone at the telephone number listed on the website, don't give up. Contact one of the local congregations and they can put you in touch with someone who knows the times that the Family History Center in that area operates. You can get a telephone number for local congregations by looking in your local white or yellow pages under the Church of Jesus Christ of Latter-day Saints. Here's a hint: since all LDS church leaders serve on a voluntary basis, doing their church work around their regular 8:00am to 5:00pm jobs, the telephone numbers listed are often only answered on Sundays or weekday evenings, when these volunteer leaders are most likely to be at the church building.

Have Patience

Finally, have patience with those who staff these Centers. Few are professional genealogists, in fact, the vast majority are not. They are individuals like you, who have a great love of genealogy and family research and want to help others have successful research experiences.

Let me stress that these Centers are open to anyone – regardless of religious belief – who have an interest in doing genealogy. In fact, records of attendance at these Centers indicate that something on the order of 60% of those who use Family History Centers are not members of the Church of Jesus Christ of Latter-day Saints.

Share Your Success

As mentioned earlier in this chapter, the Genealogical Society of Utah and the LDS Church provides these wonderful resources for genealogists the world over. They are constantly adding to their collection. And that is where you come in. If you have had success identifying ancestors through any of the LDS sources (or through any source, for that matter), please share that information with the LDS Church. It will become a part of their genealogical collection, which will in turn be available to other researchers who may be working on the same lines as you.

I have been contacted by genealogists as far away as Scotland who have gotten my name from genealogical information I had provided to the LDS church. It resulted in a new friend half a world away, and the sharing of more genealogical information between us.

FamilySearch

The LDS Church has developed an extensive genealogy website (www.familysearch.org) and database that allows individuals to gain access to the genealogical resources that the LDS Church has gathered through the years. It is called **FamilySearch**. It includes genealogical records for millions of individuals, from birth, death and marriage information to military records, census data, family histories, and much, much more. Like all other genealogical resources provided by the LDS Church, FamilySearch is available to anyone, regardless of religious affiliation.

The FamilySearch website was launched on May 24, 1999. From Day 1 it has been immensely popular – and incredibly busy. It gets roughly 14.5 million hits *each day*. Through its first three complete years of existence (at the time of this writing), it garnered over 10.3 billion hits. It has definitely positioned itself as one of the premier websites available to genealogists.

Here's how it works: As you make a request for information, FamilySearch combs its extensive records, searching for matches on the name you entered. Not only that, it even matches last names that are spelled differently but sound the same (More/Moore, Fisher/Fischer, Smith/Smythe, Meier/Meyer, etc.).

Matches on the surname (if it was a surname search) then have links to allow the researcher to learn more about the record. In most cases, a short description gives details about the information contained in the record. It may include information about dates and places of birth, parents, marriage and death information, as well as information about children.

Records in FamilySearch are divided into three important areas:

- Ancestral File
- Family History Catalog
- International genealogical Index

Ancestral File

From 1979 to 1999, members of the Church of Jesus Christ of Latter-day Saints and other researchers have contributed genealogical information to the Ancestral File. The information is in family form, as submitters complete Family Group Sheets and pedigree charts for the file. The Ancestral File contains nearly 40 million names, almost all of which have been gathered into families. It's likely that out of 40 million names, at least one of your ancestors is hiding out there.

One nice feature of the Ancestral File is that the names and contact information of individuals who submitted the information are available, so that other genealogists can coordinate research with their fellow genealogists.

The Ancestral File is accessible either via the LDS Church's genealogy website (www.familysearch.org), or on CD at each Family History Center.

Family History Library Catalog

This catalog describes all the records that are available in the Family History Library's collection. It allows genealogists to locate such genealogical records as birth, marriage and death records, family histories, census records, church records, military records and much more. The records may be in book, microfiche or microfilm format, or may even be available as computer files. The Family History Library Catalog is available on the Internet, on compact disk and on microfiche.

International Genealogical Index

The International Genealogical Index (or IGI for short) is a computer file that contains the names of over 725 million people from throughout the world. The Internet version is adding new names weekly. The names were gleaned from vital, church, and other records of individuals who were born between the early 1500s and the early 1900s. Like the Family History Library catalog, the IGI is available on the Internet, on compact disk and on microfiche.

Other Resources

In addition to these databases, FamilySearch contains several other databases, including:

- US Social Security Death Index (a computer file that contains records of deaths reported to the United States Social Security Administration. Most records start in 1962, but the file does contain a few records of deaths that happened before that date).
- Pedigree Resource File (a rapidly growing, lineage-linked computer file that contains the genealogical information for millions of individuals, family relationships and birth, marriage, and death information for millions of people). Anyone wishing to share genealogical information in this file may submit their records via the FamilySearch website.
- Vital Records Indexes (a collection of computerized databases that contains birth, christening, and marriage records from selected countries around the world).

LDS Church Checklist

___ If you are able to go to Salt Lake City, Utah to go to the Family History Library, determine what information you are seeking before you go.

___ Before you go to Salt Lake City, gather all necessary genealogical information you may need while you are at the library.

___ Familiarize yourself with the genealogical services offered by the LDS Church

___ Understand the value of Family History Centers and how to get the most out of them.

___ Prepare the names you are doing research on before you go to a Family History Center.

___ Call your local Family History Center to determine days and hours they are open.

___ Be patient with Family History Center volunteers.

___ Locate the website for FamilySearch (www.familysearch.org).

___ Familiarize yourself with the information that is available on the FamilySearch website.

Additional Resources

Parker, J. Carlyle, *Going to Salt Lake City to Do Family History Research*, Marietta Publishing Company. (January 1996)

Warren, Paula Stewart and James W. Warren, *Your Guide to the Family History Center*, Betterway Publications. (August 2001)

Warren, Paula Stewart and James W. Warren, *Making the Most of Your Research Trip to Salt Lake City*, Warren Research and Publishing. (August 2001)

11. Census Records

Do you remember your best friend from elementary school? You know – the one you could tell your deepest, darkest secrets to? The one who you could tell anything? Your best friend was the one who knew everything about you. He or she was easy to get along with, and you always enjoyed their company.

Well, let me introduce you to what may well be a genealogist's best friend: the **United States Federal Population Census**. Like your best friend from days gone by, the census has secrets to reveal to you that will be some of the very best secrets you've ever known. But these secrets are about your forefathers. The information they will share is a great beginning to just about any genealogical research project. And, like your best friend in elementary school, they are easy to get along with and are easy to understand.

Who, What, When, Where, Why & How...

Perhaps you remember from your junior high or high school days the "5 Ws" of good journalism: telling the Who, What, When, Where, Why, and How of a given situation. That is exactly what the US Census does. The Constitution of the United States called for the enumeration (census) of all of its citizens beginning in 1790 and continuing every ten years after that. The earliest censuses were little more than tally marks of the population, gathered together under the head of a family. But as the years progressed, they evolved to the point that they gathered very discrete information about each family and each family member in the United States.

Following is how censuses addressed the 5 Ws:

Who. Censuses were concerned with finding out the names of every person who lived in a certain area at a certain time. The censuses between 1790 and 1840 listed heads of family only, with tallies of all other persons in the household by age and sex. Every census since that time has included the names and ages of each and every person living at that location at that time.

What. The earliest US censuses focused on counting people only. As time went by, Congress realized that census takers could glean enormous amounts of information about the population by asking just a few additional questions. From its beginnings as a tallying system, it grew to provide such information as:

• Names, ages and sex of each person enumerated
• Race
• Occupation
• Real estate information (value, owned or rented)
• Birthplace of the individual and his / her parents
• Literacy
• Relationship to the head of the household
• Marital status and how long they had been married
• Number of children born to a mother, and how many were living at the time of the census
• Years they were a US citizen
• Language spoken
• Whether they had attended school in the last year
• Military status
• Disabilities

Imagine what a gold mine a census can be as you begin your research! I like them because they often tell me more about the individuals than just their names (things like their birthplace, occupation, infirmities, etc.). It also gathers the individuals together into families.

When. Each census took the enumeration for a given date. For example, the 1910 census captured information about every individual who was living in a particular household on April 15, 1910. Even if the census taker (also called an enumerator) didn't come by the house until October 1910, the question would be asked about those living in the house on April 15 of that year. (So – babies born after that date – even if it was before the enumerator asked the question – will not be included in the census; conversely, individuals who died after that will be included on the census.) The date varied from census to census; sometimes it is on the census page, and other times you have to do a little digging to discover the date used for enumeration purposes.

United States censuses were taken in the US every ten years between 1790 and today. Due to privacy laws, the latest census available for the public to view is the 1930 census. (By law, individual records cannot be released to the public until 72 years after the census in which they were collected.) All censuses between 1790 and 1930 are available to view and search, except the 1890 census. Tragically, the vast majority of the 1890 Census was destroyed in a fire (or by the water that was used to put out the fire!).

Where. Each census is very specific about where the people lived. The earliest censuses included the county and/or city where the family lived; later censuses included that information as well as the street addresses of the individuals.

Why. As mentioned earlier, the initial reason for censuses was to determine legislative representation and for tax purposes. But Congress soon realized that important demographic information could be compiled from the census. Hence questions about national origin, literacy and occupation gave them a snapshot of what the nation looked like.

How. Enumerators went from house to house carrying large binders or tablets with the census template. They asked whoever was at home (presumably the oldest person available – preferably the head of the household) information about each of the individuals residing in the household on a given date. Just think of the difficulty that must have been in the days before ball-point pens! From the hundreds of census pages I have looked at (all microfilmed), it appears that all enumerators were required to use pen and ink rather than pencil. Many is the time that I have imagined in my mind's eye a tired, dusty enumerator stopping at the way-out-in-the-middle-of-nowhere home of one of my ancestors and asking all those questions. (Thank you from the bottom of my heart, enumerators!)

Questions, Questions, Questions

As time went on, the census forms evolved, and additional questions that were of interest to the government were added. Following are the various questions that were asked for each census:

1790
- Head of family
- Free White Males
  - 16 and up, including head of family
  - Under 16
- Free white females
  - Including head
- All other persons
- Slaves
- County
- City

Note: No schedules are known to exist for the 1790 Census for Delaware, Georgia, Kentucky, New Jersey, Tennessee, and Virginia. It is thought that they were destroyed during the War of 1812 when the British attacked Washington. Some Virginia records are available from state enumeration records taken in 1790.

1800
- Head of family
- Free white males
  - Under 10
  - 10 to 16
  - 16 to 26
  - 26 to 45
  - 45 and over
- Free white females
  - Under 10
  - 10 to 16
  - 16 to 26
  - 26 to 45
  - 45 and over
- All others
- Slaves
- Remarks

1810
(Same as 1800)

1820
- Head of family
- Free white males
  - Under 10
  - 10 to 16
  - 16 to 18
  - 16 to 26
  - 26 to 45
  - 45 and over
- Free white females
  - Under 10
  - 10 to 16
  - 16 to 18
  - 16 to 26
  - 26 to 45
  - 45 and over
- Foreigners not naturalized
- Agriculture
- Commerce
- Manufacturers
- Free coloreds

- Slaves
- Remarks

1830
- Head of family
- Free white males
    - Under 5, 5 to 10, 10 to 15, 15 to 20, 20 to 30, 30 to 40, 40 to 50, 50 to 60, 60 to 70, 70 to 80, 80 to 90, 90 to 100, over 100
- Free white females
    - Under 5, 5 to 10, 10 to 15, 15 to 20, 20 to 30, 30 to 40, 40 to 50, 50 to 60, 60 to 70, 70 to 80, 80 to 90, 90 to 100, over 100
- Slaves
- Free colored

1840
(Same as 1830)

1850
- Name
- Age
- Sex
- Color
- Occupation
- Value of real estate
- Birthplace
- Married within year
- School within year
- Cannot read or write
- Enumeration date
- Remarks

1860
- Name
- Age
- Sex
- Color
- Occupation
- Value of real estate
- Value of personal property
- Birthplace
- Married in year
- School in year
- Cannot read or write

- Enumeration date
- Remarks

1870
- Name
- Age
- Sex
- Color
- Occupation
- Value of real estate
- Value of personal property
- Birthplace
- Father foreign born
- Mother foreign born
- Month born in census year
- School in census year
- Can't read or write
- Eligible to vote
- Date of enumeration

1880
- Name
- Color
- Sex
- Age June 1 in census year
- Relationship to head of house
- Single
- Married
- Widowed
- Divorced
- Married in census year
- Occupation
- Other information
- Can't read or write
- Place of birth
- Place of birth of father
- Place of birth of mother
- Enumeration date

1890
Note: the vast majority of the 1890 census was destroyed in a tragic fire. Only fragments remain.

1900
- Name of each person whose place of abode on June 1, 1900 was in this family
- Relation to head of family
- Sex
- Color
- Month of birth
- Year of birth
- Age
- Marital status
- Number of years married
- Mother of how many children
- Number of these children living
- Place of birth
- Place of birth of father
- Place of birth of mother
- Years of immigration to US
- Number of years in US
- Naturalization
- Occupation
- Number of months not employed
- Attended school (months)
- Can read
- Can write
- Can speak English
- Home owned or rented
- Home owned free or mortgaged
- Farm or house

1910
- Name of each person whose place of abode on April 15, 1910 was in this family
- Relation to head of family
- Sex
- Race
- Age
- Marital status
- Number of years married
- Mother of how many children
- Number of these children living
- Place of birth
- Place of birth of father
- Place of birth of mother

- Years of immigration to US
- Naturalized or alien
- Language spoken
- Occupation
- Nature of trade
- Employer, worker or own account
- Number of months not employed
- Can read and write
- Attending school
- Home owned or rented
- Home owned free or mortgaged
- Farm or house
- Civil War veteran
- Blind or deaf-mute

1920
- Name of each person whose place of abode on January 1, 1920 was in this family
- Relation to head of family
- Home owned or rented
- Home owned free or mortgaged
- Sex
- Color or race
- Age
- Marital status
- Years of immigration to US
- Naturalized or alien
- Year of naturalization
- Attending school
- Can read or write
- Place of birth
- Mother tongue
- Place of birth of father
- Mother tongue of father
- Place of birth of mother
- Mother tongue of mother
- Can speak English
- Occupation

1930
- Name of each person whose place of abode on April 1, 1930 was in this family
- Relationship of this person to the head of the family

- Home owned or rented
- Value of home, if owned, or monthly rental, if rented
- Radio set
- Does this family own a farm?
- Color or race
- Age at last birthday
- Marital condition
- Age at first marriage
- Attended school or college any time since Sept. 1, 1929
- Whether able to read or write
- Place of birth
- Place of birth of father
- Place of birth of mother
- Mother tongue (or native language) of foreign born
- Year of immigration into the United States
- Naturalization
- Whether able to speak English
- Trade, profession, or particular kind of work done
- Industry or business
- Class of worker
- Whether actually at work yesterday
- Whether a veteran of U.S. Military or naval forces
- What war or expedition
- Number of farm schedule

Soundex

If you do genealogical work at all with the US Census, you will sooner or later (probably sooner) come across a term and tool called **Soundex**. Beginning with the 1880 Census, each of the censuses has been indexed – *sort of*. (Note: only twelve southern states were Soundexed for the 1930 US Census.) The index is not the typical alphabetical index you are familiar with. Rather, the Soundex indexing system attempts to provide all the advantages of an alphabetic index, yet at the same time tries to eliminate the vagaries of spelling variations for names. For example, if you were researching the name Cronin, in a strictly alphabetic index you might miss some ancestors who spelled their name *Kronin* or *Chronin*. Once you learn how to use the Soundex system (which you'll learn if you continue reading), I think you'll agree it is a remarkably ingenious way of indexing.

Each surname is assigned a four-digit alphanumeric code. The first letter of the individual's surname is always the first letter of the Soundex code. From that point, you ignore all vowels (A, E, I, O, and U) as well as the letters H, W and Y. Then, you assign a numeric value to the next three consonants.

Soundex Coding Rules

Use the following coding scheme to determine the Soundex code for the names you are researching:

1 for the letters B, P, F, and V
2 for the letters C, S, K, G, J, Q, X and Z
3 for the letters D and T
4 for the letter L
5 for the letters M and N
6 for the letter R

Then follow these (relatively) easy Soundex rules:

1. Always use the first letter of the surname, regardless of whether it is a consonant or a vowel;

2. After the initial letter of a surname, ignore all vowels (A, E, I, O, and U) as well as the letters H, W and Y;

3. Double consonants (ll, nn, etc.) are counted as one letter;

4. Only code the first three consonants after the first letter of the name – ignore the remaining consonants;

5. If a surname does not have three consonants after the first letter of the name, the number 0 is used to fill in the rest of the code.

6. Side-by-side letters that have the same Soundex code should be counted as one letter. For example, ignore the K and S in Dickson, since C, K and S all have the same Soundex code. This applies to first and second letters in a surname also.

7. If a surname has a prefix (Van, D', Von, etc.), then code the name with and without the prefix – the indexer may have used either name for coding.

Let's do a few examples to get you used to the idea and to see how it all works:

The surname Hudson would be coded H-325:
• Ignoring the vowels, H, W, and Y, Hudson becomes *Hdsn*, and:
• H = the first letter of the surname
• 3 = the numeric code for the letter D
• 2 = the numeric code for the letter S
• 5 – the numeric code for the letter N

Note that when considering the consonants in the rest of the name, we ignore any letter H (Rule #2), but since it is the first letter of the surname, we use it in the code.

The surname Quillen would be coded Q-450:
• Ignoring the vowels and the double ll (Rules #2 and #3), Quillen becomes Qln;

• Q = the first letter of the surname;
• 4 = the numeric code for the letter L
• 5 = the numeric code for the letter N
• 0 = the numeric code when there are no other consonants (see Rule #5)

Now I don't have to concern myself with whether the name in the census record was spelled Quillan, Quillen, Quillin, or Quillon. The Soundex code for each one is Q-450.

The surname Techmeyer would be coded T-256:
• Ignoring the vowels, the H and the Y (Rule #2), Techmeyer becomes Tcmr;
• T = the first letter of the surname;
• 2 = the numeric code for the letter C
• (We ignore the H – Rule #2)
• 5 = the numeric code for the letter M
• 6 = the numeric code for the letter R

The surname See would be coded S-000
• Ignoring the vowels, See becomes S;
• S = the first letter of the surname
• 0 = the numeric code for no additional consonants (see Rule #5)
• 0 = the numeric code for no additional consonants (see Rule #5)
• 0 = the numeric code for no additional consonants (see Rule #5)

The surname Van Brederode could be coded V-516 or B-636 (see Rule #7):
• Ignoring the vowels (Rule #2), Van Brederode becomes Vnbrdrd;
• V = the first letter of the surname;
• 5 = the numeric code for the letter N
• 1 = the numeric code for the letter B
• 6 = the numeric code for the letter R

And we ignore the remaining consonants in the name (Rule #4)

OR

• Ignoring the vowels (Rule #2) and assuming the name was indexed under Brederode, Van Brederode becomes Brdrd;
• B = the first letter of the surname;
• 6 = the numeric code for the letter R
• 3 = the numeric code for the letter D
• 6 = the numeric code for the letter R

And we ignore the remaining consonant in the name (Rule #4)

Hopefully, you can begin to see the power and versatility of the Soundex system of indexing. It is not flawless, however. As seen in the above example of a word with a prefix, that can pose a problem. Native American names might also pose a problem: did the researcher assign a Soundex code for *Painted* or *Shirt* for Painted Shirt, *Sitting* or *Bull* for Sitting Bull, etc. In cases like that, just code the name both ways and search for each coding.

Once you have converted the surnames you are searching for into a Soundex code, it's time to take the next step: searching through the Soundex cards.

Soundex Cards

Armed with the Soundex code, you'll now search the Soundex rolls for a match. Indexers (WPA workers) used index cards for each name on the census, and these cards are now on one of over 2,300 microfilm rolls. Unless you want to search through every state and US territory, you need to have at least a general idea of where your ancestor lived at the time of the census you are searching. At a minimum, you'll need to know the state your ancestor is from.

Soundex cards are arranged by state, and alphabetically and numerically within each state. For example, the card for the Addams family (A-352) would follow the card for the Asher family (A-260), even though if we were indexing strictly alphabetically Addams would precede Asher.

Following is an image of a Soundex card:

YEAR: 1880 1900 1910 1920 (Circle Year) **SoundexCard**

Head of Family				E.D.	Sheet
COUNTY		LOCALITY: City, Town or Municipal District			
SOUNDEX CODE	NATURALIZED? Yes No	IMMIGRANT YEAR		NATURALIZED YEAR	
OTHER MEMBERS OF FAMILY					
NAME		RELATIONSHIP	AGE	BIRTHPLACE	

Soundex index only exists for 1880, 1900, 1910 and 1920 Censuses

While there is genealogical information on this card, you'll be tempted to stop here. But don't do that – you've come most of the way on your journey to discover your ancestor on the census, and your goal is just around the corner. In addition to the important genealogical information on the card (which helps you to determine whether or not this is the right person), you'll find (in the top right-hand corner of the card) the E.D. (Enumeration District), the census sheet, county and locality. These identification marks will enable you to go to the actual image of the census page wherein this family is listed. Also note the Soundex code in the left-center portion of the card.

Once you have found a card that seems to match the person or family you are searching for, examine it closely. If you are looking for your 2nd great grandfather and you think he was born around 1850, then the person listed on this card should have his name, an approximate age of 30 (if you are looking at a card for the 1880 census), and correct color and sex.

Note that there are only seven lines for family members on this card. Often, this won't be enough space to include all individuals living with the person listed. In those instances, another card will follow this one with the additional individuals on it. It will have the head of the family's name on it, along with the additional individuals, but it will not have the ED, volume, sheet, etc. listed.

If you believe this is the card for your ancestor, copy the information down.

The Census

Using the information from the card, you should be able to locate the exact place in the census where your ancestor is found. Once you find the correct state, search for the county that is listed on the Soundex card. (Note: If your ancestor lived in a large city, it may be listed separately from the county the city is in.) Counties are listed alphabetically, and along the left side is the information that indicates which microfilm number contains the census schedule for that area.

Obtain the microfilm roll, then using the microfilm reader, fast forward to the Enumeration District, sheet and volume number indicated on the Soundex card. Once you arrive at the page, look for the individual or family that is listed.

Write it Down!

Now that you've found your ancestor and his or her family, what next? First and foremost, write down the information exactly as it appears on the census. Writing the information down exactly is very important. For example, even though you KNOW that your great grandmother's name was *Susan,* if her name appears as *Susannah* on the census, resist the temptation to "correct" the entry when you copy the information. It may just be that the family traditions about her name being Susan are incorrect, and that her real name was Susannah.

I had an interesting experience with that in my own family. Family tradition held that my great grandmother was born in Arkansas. Yet when I located her as a child on a census schedule, it listed Texas as her state of birth. Even though I knew that wasn't right, I wrote the information down exactly as it appeared. Years later, I learned from one of my great aunts that my great grandmother's birth place really was Texas...she only told people she was born in Arkansas because she was embarrassed to admit she was born in Texas! (Sorry to those from the Lone Star state!)

Back to writing exactly what appears: write the information on a piece of paper. You can also go to the LDS Church website (www.familysearch.org) and copy any of the blank census templates that are available there. If you are lucky, the library where you are reviewing census records has a microfilm reader that also will make copies of the microfilm page you are viewing. This is the most accurate and efficient method of preserving the information. Often, a library that has 10 or 20 microfilm readers may only have one or two that can make copies. It is well worth your time to check with the librarian to see if they have a reader that makes copies, because if they do, it will save you a lot of time.

What Next?

Okay, so now you have found your great grandfather in the US Census. Now what do you do? Before you declare victory and move on – consider a caution. While the amount of information that is found in censuses is immense, remember that it is considered a secondary source of information – much of the information was written down many years after the event happened. Events like place of birth of parents, year and or months of birth, etc., could be incorrect. Consider the following *Census Conundrum* for my own great grandfather.

According to my great grandfather, Edgar Estil Quillen, he was born January 15, 1880 in Lee County, Virginia. He was the son of Jonathan Baldwin Quillen and Sarah Minerva (Burke) Quillen. Here is the critical information that several censuses contain about these individuals through the years:

1880 Census – enumerated June 1, 1880

Quillen, Jonathan B. Head of House, 35 years, born in Tennessee
    Sarah M.   Wife, 34 years old, born in Virginia
    Emmett V. Son, 9 years old, born in Virginia
    Thomas F. Son, 8 years old, born in Virginia
    Lizzie L. Daughter, 3 years old, born in Virginia
    William E. Son, 1 year old, born in Virginia

Here's my first conundrum. My great grandfather says he was born in Virginia in January 1880. Yet here is his family on June 1, 1880, and he is not listed with them, but he would have been, had he actually been born in 1880. Perhaps he was born after June 1, 1880, or on January 15, 1881.

1890 Census
Destroyed, so there was no information available for this family.

1900 Census – enumerated June 7, 1900
Quillen, Jonathan B. Head of House, born in May 1845, 55 years, born in Tennessee
> Sarah M. Wife, born September 1846, 54 years old, born in Virginia
> Lizzie L. Daughter, born April 1877, 23 years, born in Virginia
> William E. Son, born February 1879, 21 years old, born in Virginia
> Edgar E. Son, born October 1881, 18 years old, born in Virginia
> Creed C. Son, born July 1882, 17 years old, born in Tennessee
> Charles C. Son, born January 1885, 15 years old, born in Tennessee
> Henry P. Son, born September 1889, 10 years old, born in Tennessee

Conundrum # 2 – this census shows my great grandfather's birth date as October 1881, not January 1880 as my great grandfather always said. But – that explains why he wasn't found on the 1880 census. So perhaps he wasn't born in 1880 after all.

1910 Census – enumerated May 10, 1910
Quillen, Edgar E. Head of House, 28 years old, born in Virginia
> Dolly, Wife, 25 years old, born in Pennsylvania
> Lee, son, 4 years old, born in Oklahoma
> Helon, son, 3 years old, born in Oklahoma

The census says he is 28 years old on the day of enumeration (May 10, 1910). If that is true, then that would lend credence to the supposition that his birthday was probably October 1881. Had he been born in January of 1880 or 1881, the census would show his age as 30 (if he was born in 1880) or 29 (if he was born in 1881). But if he was born in October 1881, then he would have been 28 in May of 1910 – and he would have turned 29 in October 1910. Maybe we have it figured out. Let's see if the 1920 census supports that conclusion.

1920 Census – enumerated January 31, 1920
Quillen, Ed, Head of House, 39 years old, born in Tennessee
> Dolly, wife, 35 years old, born in Pennsylvania
> Lee, son, 15 years old, born in Oklahoma

Helon, son, 13 years old, born in Oklahoma
Lloyd, son, 9 years old, born in Oklahoma
Ruth, daughter, 6 years old, born in Oklahoma
Annabelle, daughter, 3 years, four months, born in Oklahoma

Okay, now this is getting a little silly. If he was born in October 1881, as we surmised from the last two censuses, then he should have been 38 on his last birthday, not 39. But if he was born in October 1880, then he would have been 39 on January 31, 1920. But that would have made the information from the last two censuses incorrect.

Just to cross us up a little bit more, his state of birth is now listed as Tennessee, not Virginia! This might explain why exhaustive searches of Virginia vital records have not turned up a birth record for him. His three younger brothers are also listed as having been born in Tennessee. Hmmm - maybe I should look in Tennessee for a birth record for him!

Here is what the 1930 Census says about the Edgar Quillen family:

1930 Census – enumerated April 2, 1930
Quillen, Ed, Head of House, 48 years old at last birthday, born in Tennessee
Dollie, wife, 46 years old at last birthday, born in Pennsylvania
Lee, son, 25 years old at last birthday, born in Oklahoma
Ruth, daughter, 16 years old at last birthday, born in Oklahoma
Annabelle, daughter, 13 years at last birthday, four months, born in Oklahoma
Lois May, daughter, 8 years old at last birthday, born in Oklahoma

Well, the conundrum continues – had my great grandfather been born in October 1881, he would have been 48 at the time of this census, not 49. It does however, support the Tennessee birthplace theory (or at least he - or whoever answered the enumerator's questions - thought that is where he was born!).

So what does all this tell us? For starters, it validates the difficulties of using only secondary sources. Secondary sources should be used as starting points to finding primary sources. They often provide wonderful clues (but some-times those clues can be misleading!). I will continue my hunt for my great grandfather's birth certificate by looking in Tennessee in October 1881. These census reports have gotten me very close to this elusive ancestor of mine, but I really want to pin down the exact date of his birth by finding a primary source.

Secondly, it points out some of the foibles of the census process. As good as it is – and in my estimation it is very good – the census process is limited by the inaccuracies of humans providing information. Enumerators asked the oldest individual they could find at home for the information. In the case of my great grandfather, an older son may have been the only one available to answer questions, and he may have assumed his father was born in Tennessee and not Virginia, and he might also have made a mistake in estimating his father's age. I suppose the possibilities for error could go on and on.

Finding the Censuses

Notwithstanding the lack of exact information, I heartily recommend that you use census records to assist you in finding families you are searching for. So, where do you find them? There are several places. If you live in the state where your ancestors lived, the genealogy section of the state library will have at least your state's census records, and they may have the records for other states. (See Appendix B for a listing of state libraries nationwide.)

If the state library doesn't have the census microfilms, then there are fourteen locations of the national archives, and each has all the states' censuses on microfilm. The addresses, phone numbers, and websites for the centers are listed on pages 61-64 in chapter 8, *Genealogical Collections & Libraries*.

Hours vary from center to center. Generally, all offices are open Monday through Friday during normal business hours. Most offer at least one evening a week where they are open until 8:00pm and most are also open at least one if not two Saturdays per month. Before you go, call ahead or check each library's website for specific information about their hours of operation.

Finally, don't forget that your local Family History Center also allows you to order and view census microfilms from the Family History Library in Salt Lake City.

Mortality Schedules

Another important record that was kept coincident with the US Census was the Mortality Schedule for the 1850 through 1880 censuses. These schedules listed everyone who had died between June 1 of the year before the census and May 31 of the census year. They listed the name, age, sex, marital status, race, occupation, birthplace, cause of death and length of illness for each individual who passed away during that year.

If you have an opportunity to search Mortality Schedules, you may find it interesting to note the ages of those who died. So many of them are children under age 10 - infant and young child mortality was very high in the mid-1800s. I guarantee it will tug at your heartstrings.

Census Records Checklist

___ Find the location of the nearest facility that has US Census records.

___ Determine which surnames you want to search for.

___ Determine the name of the head of household if not the ancestor you are looking for.

___ Know the approximate birth year of the ancestors you are searching for.

___ Try and discover the family's place of residence during the census year

___ Review the Soundex process, and develop the Soundex code for the ancestors you want to search for.

___ If possible, identify the names of siblings and parents of the ancestors you are searching for (this will help you identify the correct family).

___ Be sure and have pen and paper to record information found.

___ Obtain blank census templates to enter information you find (you can e-mail me and I'll send them to you).

Additional Resources

Carlberg, Nancy Ellen, *Beginning Census Research*, Carlberg Press (January 1992)

Dollarhide, William, *The Census Book: A Genealogist's Guide to Federal Census Facts, Schedules and Indexes*, Heritage Quest (1999)

12. Military Records

The information found in military records is an often-overlooked gold mine for genealogists. Information I have gleaned from pension records has enabled me to piece families together, and records of military service have made my ancestors seem like real people to me. And I suspect, with just a little effort on your part, you may have many of the same experiences. Read on and you'll get a few clues on how best to find your ancestors among the military records of our nation.

Motivation

The motivation for your ancestors' military service is as varied as the individuals who enlisted. It may have been for glory's sake, or to answer the call of their country to fight against oppression. It may have been a burning desire to abolish (or prolong) slavery, or merely to earn a paycheck and a roof (albeit canvas) over their heads during difficult economic times. Whatever the motivation, it is clear that many American men in past generations served in the military.

American Wars

In her storied history, Americans have fought in a number of wars. If you are not sure whether one of your ancestors fought, see if they were of military age (roughly 16 to 35) during any of these wars:

• French and Indian Wars (1754 to 1763)
• Revolutionary War (1775 to 1783)
• War of 1812 (1812 to 1815)
• Mexican War (1846 to 1848)
• Civil War (1861 to 1865)
• Spanish-American War (1898)

- Philippine War (1899 to 1902)
- World War I (1917 to 1918)
- World War II (1941 to 1945)
- Korean Conflict (1950 to 1953)
- Vietnam War (1965 to 1973)

If they were of military age during any of those wars, it may well be worth your time to check out military records for genealogical information.

Where to Begin
First of all, decide what you want to know for whom. Perhaps your interest is in whether or not an ancestor served in the military, and if so, what battles he was engaged in. Or perhaps you really don't care about that, but would like to glean any genealogical information about that particular ancestor that might be included in military records.

When beginning your search, use common sense. If you are trying to find information from military records about an ancestor that was born in 1855, you probably won't find him listed in enlistment or service records for him during the Civil War! (However, you may find him mentioned in a pension application by his father or his widowed mother. More on that later.)

Let's use my third great grandfather as an example. Leonidas Horney was born in 1817. That would have made him the ripe old age of 44 at the time the Civil War broke out in 1861. Was he too old to participate in the Civil War? Perhaps. But it also put him at about the age of senior military officers. So, I might as well check Civil War military records to see if he may have served. Another possibility is that he may have served during the Mexican War. So I should check those records also.

In Leonidas' case, I had a bit of a clue, in that I have a picture of him in a Union Civil War uniform. I also knew that family tradition held that he had enlisted in Missouri. So as a shot in the dark, I got on the Internet and entered *Missouri Civil War Records*. I received 234,000 hits to my request and selected the first one: *Index to the Civil War in Missouri*. Once I got to the website, one of the options was *Index to Officers in Missouri Military Units*. I selected that, and within seconds had the following information:

Leonidas Horney, original commission: Captain, 10th Missouri Cavalry
    Subsequent promotions:
    Major 10th Missouri Cavalry
    Lieutenant Colonel 10th Missouri Cavalry.

This was important information. While it might not look like genealogical information, it provides me an important element in researching military records – his military unit. Many US military records were kept by military unit.

The National Archives

At some point in your search for the military records of your ancestors, you will cross paths with the National Archives of the United States of America. The repository of all military records, the National Archives will likely yield you a great deal of genealogical information, if you only know (or learn) how to use them. The National Archives has the following military records available for research:

• Volunteer military service (1775 to 1902)
• US Army military records (1789 to 1917)
• US Navy records (1798 to 1902)
• US Marine Corps (1789 to 1904)
• US Coast Guard and its predecessors (Revenue Cutter, Life Saving Services, and Bureau of Lighthouses) (1791 to 1919)
• Civil War Service and pension records (Union as well as Confederate)

Here are the types of records available:

Enlistment Records

Enlistment records of soldiers can be very interesting. At a minimum, they will tell you the name, rank, date and place that the individual enlisted. They may also tell you such interesting tidbits as their occupation, age, physical description (height, weight, hair and eye color, complexion, size of hands and feet, etc.) and marital status.

Compiled Military Service Records (CMSR)

Every volunteer soldier has had compiled for him a Compiled Military Service Record (CMSR) for each regiment he served in. It contains basic information about his service career while in that regiment. Information contained within the record might be enlistment information, leave (vacation) requests, muster (roll call) records, and injury or illness reports. If he was killed in action, this will most likely be found in the record, or information about his discharge if he survived.

When I requested the service record for Colonel Leonidas Horney, my third great grandfather, I received documents that included the following:

• The date and place of his enlistment;
• His date of birth;
• His height, hair and eye color and color of complexion;
• The rank he enlisted as;
• The name of his regiment and company;
• The commanders he reported to;

- Several muster sheets showing his presence on specific dates (muster sheets are like roll calls);
- A copy of a letter from his commanding officer granting him a two-month leave;
- Several documents detailing his promotion from Captain to Major to Lieutenant Colonel;
- Two casualty sheets, one detailing a slight injury sustained at the Battle of Corinth and the other reporting his death in the Battle of Champion Hill, Mississippi on May 16, 1863.

Pension Records

Pensions were applied for by Union army soldiers, their widows and / or their minor children. Because of the need to ensure that the applicant was indeed related to the former soldier, a great deal of information was often requested to substantiate the relationship. A widow, for example, would have had to provide the date and place of their marriage (and often the name of the person who performed the marriage). She would often be required to provide either the marriage certificate, or a certified record signed by the minister who performed the ceremony. If the widow had children under the age of 16, she also needed to provide proof of their birth in the form of a birth certificate, or a government-certified document that provided the child's name, birth date and birth place – all genealogical nuggets.

Pension files are all indexed by the **National Archives and Records Administration** (NARA), and the index is available at National Archives locations or at the following website: www.archives.gov/research_room/genealogy/military/pension_index_1861_to_1934.html

When I searched for the pension record for one of my ancestors who served in the military and fought in the Civil War, I found a plethora of information about him and his family. After his death, his widow completed a series of affidavits that contained the following information:

- Her full maiden name;
- Her age and birth date;
- Her birth place;
- The date and place she married her husband;
- The name of the person who performed their marriage ceremony;
- The names, birth dates and ages of all their children 16 years of age and younger;
- The names and birth dates of those children who had died.

This is truly a treasure trove of genealogical information.

Record of Events

Generally, not much of genealogical value is listed in the Records of Events. They are generally sort of journal entries that trace the movement of troops. Often, they are little more than places and dates that the various companies and regiments were stationed or marching to.

These would be of interest if you wanted to trace an ancestor's movements through the war. In the case of the Civil War, it would be interesting to see if any of your ancestors engaged in battles against one another. Numerous of my family lines lived in and around border states during the Civil War, and both the Confederate and Union armies had members of my family fighting for them.

Confederate Records

A special note about Confederate army records. Both Compiled Military Service Records (CMSR) and Records of Events were kept for Confederate units. They are often not as complete as Union records of the same type, as many Confederate records did not survive the war. Pensions were granted to Confederate veterans and their widows and minor children by the states of Alabama, Arkansas, Florida, Georgia, Kentucky, Louisiana, Mississippi, Missouri, North Carolina, Oklahoma, South Carolina, Tennessee, Texas, and Virginia. Note that it was the *states* who granted these pensions, not the federal government; those records are contained in the State Archives of the state where the veteran resided after the war, not in the National Archives.

Bounty Land Warrants

The Continental Congress discovered a way to pay its veterans or their widowed and orphaned dependents by giving them cash or (preferably) public lands. Laws passed between 1776 and 1855 authorized granting warrants for land to those who had served in the Revolutionary War, the War of 1812, the Indian Wars and the Mexican War.

The documents in a Bounty Land Warrant file are similar to those contained in pension files. They are particularly rich in genealogical data if it is the widow or children of the veteran who applied for the Bounty Land Warrant.

Other Resources

As you begin to plow the fertile ground of military records in search of your ancestors, understand that that there are far more records available than I can possibly list in this book. Veterans' census records, indexes to old soldiers' homes, indexes for soldiers' cemeteries, and Veterans' societies are just a few of the other resources that are available. The Church of Jesus Christ of Latter-day Saints has published a research outline for military records that gives an excellent overview of the records that are available to researchers: *US Military*

Records – Research Outline, Intellectual Reserve, Inc. It is available through the LDS Church Distribution Center in Salt Lake City, Utah (Tel. 800/537-5950) for a small fee.

Okay – So Where Do I Find These Wonderful Records?

While some of the records we have been discussing have been microfilmed, most have not. Your first stop should be to either a regional National Archives site (see the list at the end of Chapter 8 on *Libraries*), or perhaps to your local Family History Center. They will have indexes that will help you determine whether or not your ancestor's records are part of those that have been microfilmed or not. If they have been microfilmed, then you may be able to view them at the location you are at.

In all probability, however, you will not be able to view the records at the regional National Archives center you are at or even at the Family History Center. You have several options. The first option is to visit the National Archives site in Washington DC. If that is not practical or possible – don't fret – you may write and request photocopies of the records. You'll need to obtain a number of copies of the National Archives Trust Fund (NATF) Form 85 for Pensions and Bounty Land Warrants and Form 86 for Military Service Records. These forms are available for free upon request. You may order the forms by writing to:

National Archives and Records Administration
Attn: NWCTB
700 Pennsylvania Avenue, NW
Washington, DC 20408-0001
Website: www.archives.gov/global_pages/inquire_form.html#part_a.

Each form (one per soldier or sailor) should be filled out with as much information as you have on the individual, but at least with his complete name, the war he fought in, and the state where he enlisted. If you know his regiment or company, include that also. The form should then be submitted to the National Archives address above.

Because federal law requires all such requests for information to be accompanied by a signature, forms must either be mailed or faxed.

The National Archives personnel simply do not have the time available to conduct extensive research for individuals, and for that reason it is important to provide as much information about the soldier as you can, so that they can determine without error that they have found the right soldier and records. If the request isn't clear enough, they may reject the request, asking for more information, or they may copy all the records of the soldiers they think might fit the request you sent.

The Internet and Military Records

I know there is an entire chapter on doing genealogy on the Internet in this book. But I felt like it was still worth giving a special mention in this chapter. The advent of the Internet has increased access to (and knowledge of!) a multitude of resources, including military records. I began scouring military records in the late 1970s and early 1980s – prior to the general proliferation of the Internet. In those days, the process was:

Request a form via mail.
Wait.
Complete and mail the form.
Wait.
Receive a rejection.
Sigh.
Complete another form and mail it.
Wait.

But the Internet has collapsed the above weeks- or months-long process to a matter of moments in many cases. The example I used earlier in the chapter about Leonidas Horney was not a true example...I had performed that search in the 1980s for him. At that time, it took around five weeks to get the same information that I received within literally 30 or 40 seconds on the Internet. That's powerful!

Military Records Search Checklist

____ Identify an ancestor you think may have served in the military.

____ Decide what you want to learn.

____ Understand what military records are available to research.

____ Determine (if possible) the branch of service in which your ancestor served.

____ Understand the process for obtaining records (Internet, mail request, personal visit).

____ Select a record to search.

____ Request Form 85 or 86, complete and mail to the National Archives for your ancestor.

Additional Resources

Beers, Henry Putney, *The Confederacy: A Guide to the Archives of the Confederate States of America*, Smithsonian Institution Press, (August 1986)

General Index to Pension Files 1861–1934, National Archives and Records Administration Microfilm Publication T288.

Hewett, Janet B., editor, *The Roster of Union Soldiers, 1861 – 1865*, 33 volumes. Wilmington, North Carolina, Broadfoot Publishing, 1997.

Intellectual Reserve, Inc., *US Military Records – Research Outline* (a publication of the Church of Jesus Christ of Latter-day Saints)

Johnson, Richard S., *How to Locate Anyone Who is or Has Been in the Military*, 7th edition, Fort Sam Houston, Texas: Military Information Enterprises, 1996.

Military Service Records in the National Archives of the United States, National Archives and Records Administration (pamphlet produced by the NARA).

US War Department, *The War of Rebellion: A Compilation of the Official Records of the Union and Confederate Armies,* reprint: Gettysburg, Pennsylvania, The National Historical Society.

13. Ethnic Research

America is the great melting pot where people of all nations have emigrated. In the stew of her population are a seemingly limitless number of ethnic groups, and individuals within those groups that are interested in tracing their ancestors. Massive efforts to microfilm records from all over the world have made previously unavailable documents available at the click of a mouse through the power of the Internet. Individuals no longer need to expend the time or money to travel to the lands of their ancestors' nativity to conduct their research.

African-American Research

In recent years, great strides have been made in the area of African-American research. One of the quintessential books on the topic was written by Dee Parmer Woodtor. It is called *Finding a Place Called Home: A Guide to African-American Genealogy and Historical Identity*, and it is an excellent resource for genealogists of African-American roots.

The search for the first 135 years or so (back to 1870) is basically the same for African-Americans as it is for other ethnic groups. First of all, start with your parents, grandparents and if you're lucky enough – your great grandparents. Get the facts – when and where they were born and married, the names of their parents and siblings and vital information on each of them. Don't forget to visit with your aunts and uncles too to verify this information, or to find and hopefully resolve areas of discrepancy. Also, look for clues – and write them down – that might shed light on your pre-1870 family history.

Family traditions are important, but be willing to take them for what they are – clues to finding very small needles in very large haystacks. If the family tradition is that your 2nd great grandfather was a slave on a plantation in Mississippi and that he ran away and was caught and returned several times, consider it helpful to your research, but not necessarily the gospel truth. Generally speaking, even in stories that may have been most embellished by dimming memories through the years, there is often a kernel of truth in them. Maybe your 2nd great grandpa didn't run away three times, but perhaps he did run away once. And that clue might be just the one you need to identify this ancestor in an era when accurate and specific records weren't kept.

It seems to me that successful researchers of African-American ancestry need to have a higher degree of "detectivism" than other genealogists. All genealogists seem to possess a bit of this attribute, but it needs to be higher in researchers of African-American roots. America was not as good about keeping vital statistics (census, immigration, birth, death and marriage records, for example) on slaves. So that requires a little more creativity, a little deeper digging in non-traditional genealogical resources. And sometimes a combination of records needs to be researched and compared:

• 1850 and 1860 slave schedules
• Census records
• Civil War enlistment records
• Deeds
• Family Bible records
• Family histories and traditions
• Freedmen's Bureau records
• Letters
• Obituaries
• Old newspapers
• Plantation records
• Probate records
• Wills

Don't forget obituaries in your search for these elusive ancestors (actually, it's not the ancestors that are elusive, it's their records). True – the original records of the individuals being sought may be sketchy – if in existence at all. However, an obituary might shed immense light on your research. An ancestor born in 1850 who died at age 75 in 1925 may have important information revealed in his or her obituary. Perhaps it tells where and when he was born, names of children and/or parents and the name of his wife. It may reveal the state – or states – of the plantations where he was held in slavery. While obituaries are considered secondary genealogical resources, they may also be the only sources available, or perhaps may lead you to the location of other records that might be checked.

The obituary may help you pinpoint a place to search, and maybe even a timeframe. From there you can check local slave records, the appropriate slave schedules and perhaps even records of the plantation owner.

You may scratch your head about the suggestion to search Civil War enlistment records, but several hundred thousand slaves enlisted in the northern army. Records of these individuals were kept that may shed light on an ancestor or two.

In addition to Ms. Woodtor's book mentioned at the beginning of this section, there are several other excellent books on African-American genealogy. Look for *Black Roots: A Beginners Guide to Tracing the African-American Family Tree* by Tony Burroughs (Fireside Books) and *How to Trace Your African-American Roots: Discovering Your Unique History* by Barbara Thompson Howell (Citadel Printing). Both are excellent resources to help you begin searching for your African-American ancestors.

As mentioned earlier in this book, I have found genealogical societies to be immense helps to me in my personal research, and you may find that to be the case for your research. There are several genealogical societies dedicated to assisting in the search for African-American roots. Among the most active are:

Afro-American Historical and Genealogical Society, Inc.
PO Box 73067
Washington, D.C. 20056-3067
www.rootsweb.com/~mdaahgs/

The Afro-American Historical and Genealogical Society, Inc. is a non-profit organization dedicated to preserving the history of African-Americans. They encourage active participation in genealogy and recording your findings so that others may benefit from your work. Membership in the organization is $35 for an individual or $40 for a family, and includes copies of the semi-annual *Journal of the Afro-American Historical and Genealogical Society* and the bi-monthly *AAHGS News*.

As of this writing, local chapters exist in 17 of the 50 states. Perhaps you would be interested in forming a local chapter if your state isn't currently represented. If so, the website lists its officers under the *Organization* tab, and there are several officers who serve as *Chapter Establishment* members.

African-American Genealogy Group
PO Box 1798
Philadelphia, PA 19105-1798
www.aagg.org

While primarily focused on individuals who live in the Philadelphia area, the African-American Genealogy Group is nonetheless a valuable resource for those searching their African-American roots. Membership in the organization is $25 annually, and includes a subscription to their quarterly newsletter. A section of their website is dedicated for members to share their research in 17 southern and eastern states, including Alabama, Delaware, Florida, Georgia,

Kentucky, Louisiana, Maryland, Mississippi, New Jersey, New York, North Carolina, Pennsylvania, South Carolina, Tennessee, Virginia, Washington DC and West Virginia.

The Schomburg Center for Research in Black Culture
515 Malcolm X Boulevard
New York, NY 10037-1801
www.nypl.org/research/sc/sc.html

The Schomburg Center for Research in Black Culture is devoted to collecting, preserving, and providing access to resources documenting the experiences of peoples of African descent throughout the world. Much broader than just a genealogical site, it nonetheless can be a source of assistance to African-American researchers.

Here are a few websites that you should peruse in your quest to find your African-American ancestors:

The AfriGeneas website can be found at **www.afrigeneas.com**. The home page of the website declares its purpose as: "...devoted to African-American genealogy, to researching African ancestry in the Americas in particular and to genealogical research and resources in general. It is also an African Ancestry research community featuring the AfriGeneas mail list, the AfriGeneas message boards and daily and weekly genealogy chats..."

The Afro-Louisiana History and Genealogy website can be found at **www.ibiblio.org/laslave**. Among other things, it provides a searchable database which contains background on 100,000 slaves who were brought to Louisiana in the 18th and 19th centuries. So if your roots go back to Louisiana, this is a website you definitely want to check out.

AOL has a Genealogy Forum website – **www.genealogyforum.com** – that is helpful to those researching their African-American roots. From the home page, click on any of several topics, and you'll be taken to a link that may be of use to you. Click on the *Messages* icon and you'll be taken to a message board where individuals are posting information about various individuals. Perhaps you'll find one of your ancestors hiding there. Under the same icon, look for *Ethnic Resources*, and click on *African-American Resources*, and you'll be whisked to a host of new websites specializing in African-American research.

Native American Research
Another tough area of genealogy is that of searching for your Native American roots. As with African-American genealogy, once you get back past the 1870s it becomes increasingly more difficult to do research in this area.

Prior to that time, the research process is pretty much the same as that for individuals researching other ethnic roots: start with what you know, expand that to what your parents and grandparents and other relatives know, and work your way back in history. Gather all the documentary evidence you can: birth and death certificates, marriage certificates, etc. In addition to being important primary sources, they may shed light on areas that you thought you had no information. They may identify a relative or birthplace that was heretofore unknown to you.

When researching Native American roots, knowing the tribal affiliation of your ancestors is critical. This will be a key element in your search.

If you can identify an ancestor who was living at the turn of the 20th century, you are in luck. Because if they were enumerated by census takers in the 1900 or 1910 Census, an additional page of information was completed for all Native Americans. Included were questions that identified the following:

• Other name (Indian name) of this Indian
• Tribe of this Indian
• Tribe of the father of this Indian
• Tribe of the mother of this Indian
• Has this Indian any white blood? (The 1910 Census asked for percentage of white, Indian and Black blood)
• Is this Indian, if married, living in polygamy?
• Was this Indian living on their own land? (1910 only)
• The type of dwelling this Indian is living in (civilized or aboriginal dwelling?)
• Graduated from which educational institution (1910 only)

These questions were included in a section of the census called *Special Inquiries Relating to Indians,* and as you can see, the questions it asked provided helpful genealogical information. Answers to any of those questions will provide you with yet another piece of information to continue your search.

Another great source for Native American genealogical research are the **Dawes Rolls**. Henry Dawes was a US Senator who was appointed Commissioner of Indian Affairs. On February 8, 1887, the Dawes Act was passed by Congress and provided for the allotment of land to Native Americans of the Five Civilized Tribes living in Indian Territory (Oklahoma and Texas) on the following basis:

• To each head of a family, one quarter of a section (160 acres)
• To each single person over eighteen years of age, one-eighth of a section (80 acres)
• To each orphan child over eighteen years of age, one-eighth of a section (80 acres)

• To each living child under the age of eighteen, one-sixteenth of a section (40 acres)

The enrollment process took place between 1898 and 1906. The census was for people of the Cherokee, Choctaw, Chickasaw, Creek and Seminole tribes. Individuals were placed into the following categories:

• Citizens by blood
• Citizens by marriage (usually whites; the code used to identify these individuals was IW – meaning "intermarried whites")
• New born citizens by blood
• Minor citizens by blood
• Freedmen (former slaves of the Indians who were adopted into the tribes)
• New born freedmen
• Minor freedmen

The Dawes Act was viewed with suspicion by many Native Americans at the time of its passage. They were concerned that it was an elaborate method to identify and then relocate them (again). Nevertheless, many ventured forth and signed up. Many did not (can you blame them?).

Controversial or not, the Dawes Rolls provide 634 pages of double-columned, single-space typed list that provides the names, sex, age, tribal affiliation and percent of Indian blood for each individual. There are a number of websites where you can learn more about the Dawes Act and learn how to order copies of the allotment schedules. At the time of this writing, they could be purchased for as little as $25. One very informative website is **www.netmodem.com/dawes**. They are also available to view on microfilm at your local Family History Center. (Remember – the LDS Church charges only a minor shipping and handling cost to have microfilms delivered to local Family History Centers where they can be viewed for six weeks.)

Another enrollment effort for the Native Americans living in Indian Territory in the late 1800s and early 1900s was the **Guion Miller Roll**. Focused exclusively on the Cherokee tribe, the rolls contain important genealogical information. Growing out of one of the darkest chapters of US history, the Guion Miller Roll lists the names of Cherokees who were descendants of the individuals who participated in the 1835-1836 Trail of Tears – the forced relocation of the Cherokee Nation. Applicants needed to establish a link between them and those who were relocated. Over 45,000 applications were filed, listing over 90,000 individuals, so this is a rich source indeed. Information about the Guion Miller Roll can be found on several websites, one of the most informative being **www.rootsweb.com/~cherokee/miller.html**.

The index for the Guion Miller Roll can be accessed at **www.archives.gov/research_room/arc/arc_info/native_americans_guion_miller_index.html**.

If you find the names of an ancestor (or ancestors), you may order a copy of their application. The applications are contained on nearly 350 rolls of microfilm, and each application contains a great deal of genealogical information. Remember, individuals trying to prove their descent from those who walked the Trail of Tears must have demonstrated their familial connection to them. You should therefore be able to move at least two or three generations further along your family tree through these efforts.

There are several sources where you can order copies of applications. Again, your local LDS Family History Center is one source. Another is **The Indian Territory Genealogical and Historical Society**, c/o John Vaughn Library NSU, Tahlequah, Oklahoma 74464. To get a copy of the application from the ITGHS, send $5.00 and include a large, self-addressed and stamped envelope with your request. Your request should list the name of the applicant and his/her application number.

Cherokee Connections (Genealogical Publishing Company) by Myra Vanderpool Gormley is an excellent resource for those of Cherokee descent. It is focused on assisting individuals to establish their heritage for tribal membership. A side benefit is that it is a great book for those who are merely looking to extend that which they know about their lineage. It provides more details on the Dawes and Guion Miller Rolls, and points out other sources of research.

Another well-written and excellent resource is Bob Blankenship's *Cherokee Roots* (Cherokee Roots Publishing). Mr. Blankenship covers the US Censuses of the Cherokee Nation between 1817 and 1924. A two-volume set, the first volume covers those who lived east of the Mississippi River, and the second volume covers those members of the Cherokee tribe who lived west of the river.

AOL has a Genealogy Forum website – **www.genealogyforum.com** – that is helpful to those researching their Native American roots. From the home page, click on any of several topics, and you'll be taken to a link that may be of use to you. Click on the *Messages* icon and you'll be taken to a message board where individuals are posting information about various individuals. Perhaps you'll find one of your ancestors hiding there. Under the same icon, look for *Ethnic Resources*, and click on *Native American Resources*, and you'll be whisked to a host of new websites specializing in Native American research.

Jewish Research

A wealth of information is available (if you know where to find it!) for those searching for their Jewish ancestors. As with all genealogical research and as has been stated before – start with what you know. Record all that you know, then poll parents, grandparents and other living relatives. Glean all the names, dates, places, copies of birth, marriage and death certificates that you can. Look especially for old letters, obituaries and journals.

Moving beyond individuals that you know, the common sources of genealogical research come into the picture: censuses, vital statistics records kept by government offices and churches, etc. I would suggest that you go from general population records (like censuses that enumerated all individuals in the population) to records created specifically for (and often by) those of Jewish ancestry. Begin your research using the genealogy strategies and methods for the area where your family is from.

There are a number of genealogical resources specific to Jewish ancestry. Some of these sources are:

- **Holocaust Records** – many records were kept on those who were imprisoned and murdered during the Holocaust. These records often assist researchers in their quest.
- **Mohel books** – books kept by *mohels* (circumcisers) of the work they performed. Remember, Jewish law requires that male children be circumcised when they are eight days old – which should allow you to calculate birth dates of the circumcised fairly easily. Needless to say, this will be helpful for your male ancestors only.
- **Shtetl Finders** – Shtetls are Jewish towns or communities, mostly found in eastern Europe. Shtetl Finders help identify these communities, many of which have ceased to exist.
- **Yizkor Books** – these are memorial books published by Holocaust survivors from specific towns or regions. Many of the books were written in Yiddish or Hebrew. However many translations are available. They often include the history of the communities, the memories of the communities' survivors and information about families that had no one survive the Holocaust. Generally, a listing of victims are included, along with the names and addresses of those who survived.

Perhaps because of the strong family ties of Jewish people, there are many resources available to Jewish genealogists that focus on Jews. Through the years, there seems to have been immense interest in recording information about Jewish life, traditions and families. That's the good news. The bad news is that there seem to be so many options available to researchers that it is difficult to decide which to begin with. Make no mistake – searching for your Jewish roots will provide many opportunities for you to use the sleuth-like capabilities you have (or will) develop as a genealogist.

If I were researching Jewish ancestors, after I had gotten all I could from living family members, I believe I would start with **www.jewishgen.com**. It is a wonderful, well-thought-out website dedicated to Jewish genealogy. It gives you practical advice, counsel and direction. It defines terms for you, answers frequently asked questions, and is the portal to other links and databases that will assist you immensely in your search. Here are some of the highlights of this website:

- *Jewishgen Discussion Group* – this is an e-mail facilitated discussion group that encourages Jewish researchers to share the information they have, methods that have been successful for them in their research, case studies and ideas.
- *Jewishgen Special Interest Group mailing lists* – similar to the Discussion Group, this area focuses on specific areas (geographical or topical) and allows researchers to share the information they have, or to ask questions of those who have researched these specific areas. While not a complete list, at the time of this writing it included places like Belarus, Bohemia-Moravia, Denmark, Germany, Hungary, Latin America, Latvia and Romania. It also included topics such as Rabbinic ancestry, Yizor books, Shtetl (Jewish communities), genetic genealogy, etc.
- *The Jewishgen Family Finder* – a database of over 300,000 Jewish surnames. It is a database of ancestral towns and surnames currently being researched by Jewish genealogists worldwide. Researchers can search records submitted by others as well as submit your own surnames and towns.
- *ShtetLinks* – an infobase of over 200 stetls – Jewish communities.
- *Yizkor Book Project* – this area of the website is dedicated to unlocking the treasures that are contained in Yizkor Books. Memorials to the fallen Jews of the Holocaust, the Project is aimed at providing translation services (many Yizkor Books were originally written in Yiddish or Hebrew) and indexing work to more quickly identify individuals whose names are contained in the books.
- *Family Tree of the Jewish People* – this is a compilation of the family trees of Jewish researchers. At last count, it included the names and familial connections of over two million people.

As you can see, JewishGen is a website of immense capability and possibilities for those searching their Jewish roots.

Another outstanding website that serves as a superb resource for Jewish genealogical research is **www.feefhs.org** (PO Box 510898, Salt Lake City, Utah 84151-0898). The **Federation of East European Family History Societies** (FEEFHS) is an extremely active genealogical organization focused on researching the lives and histories of the people of eastern Europe, which of course includes many of Jewish ancestry. It is a conglomerate of heritage societies, archives, libraries, family groups and others who are researching their eastern European roots.

Another website with extensive information about Jewish research is that of the **LDS Church**. The LDS Church has an extensive Jewish collection, all of which is available to researchers through the Family History Library in Salt Lake City, or the local Family History Centers, branches of the Family History Library. To learn what sources are available, go to **www.familysearch.org**. From the home page, click on *Search the Family History Catalog for Records and Resources* link (it is found on the middle right-hand side of the page). From that link, select *Subject Search*, and type in Jewish. You'll be immediately rewarded for your efforts with a list of links to genealogical information specific to Jews. At the time of this writing, there were over 60 databases that contained information on Jewish research, including the Holocaust, cemeteries, biographies, newspapers and orphanages.

As mentioned throughout this book, the LDS Church's research facilities and records are available to all people interested in genealogy, regardless of religion.

AOL has a Genealogy Forum website **(www.genealogyforum.com)** that is helpful to those researching their Jewish roots. From the home page, click on any of several topics, and you'll be taken to a link that may be of use to you. Click on the *Messages* icon and you'll be taken to a message board where individuals are posting information about various individuals. Perhaps you'll find one of your ancestors hiding there. Under the same icon, look for *Ethnic Resources*, and click on *Jewish Resources*, and you'll be whisked to a host of new websites specializing in Jewish research.

Special Issues in Jewish Research

It seems like almost all ethnic groups have their own special research issues to deal with, and those searching Jewish ancestors are no different. Here are a few of the more prominent ones to be aware of:

• Surnames. In many parts of the world, Jews did not used fixed surnames until such usage was mandated by the government where they lived. In many instances, this was not until the late 1700s or even as late as the mid-1800s. This will of course add a certain element of difficulty to Jewish research. Prior to this, patronymics were used (the father's name was used as well as the child's given name), as well as names derived from occupations, places or even affiliation with animals. Hence the derivation of surnames like *Abramson* (Abram's son), *Schneider* (German for Tailor) or *Haas* (German for rabbit). These patronymics eventually evolved into surnames.

• The Holocaust was a tragic chapter in the history of the world and had an indelible impact on Jews and Jewish research. Entire families were wiped out, communities razed and records destroyed. There are many records that have been spawned by the Holocaust, including concentration camp records, death lists from extermination camps, Yizkor Books and others. These records help bridge the gap created by the events of the Holocaust.

• Governments often restricted the names Jews could use. Hebrew or Old Testament names were often specifically excluded, so Jews in those parts of the world often chose Yiddish or German names that had a symbolic association with an outlawed name.

Jewish Archival Research

Throughout the world, libraries and genealogical societies have collected (and are collecting) and are striving to preserve valuable genealogical information in the form of books, family histories, Yizkor Books, etc. There are a number of very active and very strong such organizations that focus primarily on Jewish archiving. Some of those organizations follow.

YIVO Institute for Jewish Research
Center for Jewish History
15 West 16th Street
New York, NY 10011

The YIVO Institute is one of the most respected archival organizations in the world. Their collection of records pertinent to Jewish research is impressive and second to none.

Yad Vashem Martyrs and Heroes
Remembrance Authority
PO Box 3477
91034 Jerusalem
Israel

Yad Vashem is dedicated to collecting and preserving information about the victims and survivors of the Holocaust. Their collection includes over 85,000 related to the Holocaust, including the world's largest library of yizkor books. Included at Yad Vashem are records that identify more than three million Jews who perished in the Holocaust.

Family History Library
35 North West Temple
Salt Lake City, Utah 84150
(*Tel. 801/240-2331*)

As detailed earlier in this section, the Family History Library of the LDS Church has a significant Jewish collection. The LDS Church has also developed a concise primer for Jewish genealogical research called *Research Outline: Jewish Genealogy*. This 38-page document will help you get started on researching your Jewish ancestors. It is available through the Church Distribution Center in Salt Lake City, Utah (Tel. 800/537-5950). The cost is minimal but the information is extensive.

Hispanic Research

Although Hispanic research does not seem to be as well developed as that for other groups, it has been assisted in recent years by the development of several excellent websites. The first of these is **home.att.net/~Alsosa** (note that you do not use a www. prefix for this website). The brainchild of Al Sosa, the website is home for the **Hispanic Genealogy Forum**, a consortium of individuals who are actively seeking their Hispanic roots and are willing to share the fruits of their labors. Al is a gentleman who had a driving passion to learn more about his Hispanic roots. But more than that, he had a passion to share his passion. Primarily through his efforts, this website has come about.

The website is a great starting point, because it offers advice, counsel and direction in a variety of areas, and is especially helpful in putting beginning genealogists' feet on the right path. It starts off very basic, by giving you a tutorial on the terms *Latin* vs. *Hispanic*, getting started in Hispanic research, a nice section on the origin of many Hispanic names, etc. It also provides a recommendation of books and other websites that will be of assistance.

Other helpful websites include:

- **www.hispanicgenealogy.com** – the website of the Hispanic Genealogy Center, an Hispanic genealogical society of New York. It includes a number of features, including multiple message boards where you can post requests for information about a relative you simply cannot find.
- **www.hispanicgen.org** is the website for the National Society of Hispanic Genealogy. This genealogy society focuses on the ancestry and culture of Spanish-speaking peoples in the southwestern United States in the areas formerly known as New Spain and Mexico (primary links cover Colorado and New Mexico). Links to a large variety of Hispanic genealogy sites, message boards and special topics are listed on the website. You can also contact the society at National Society of Hispanic Genealogy, 924 West Colfax Avenue, Suite 104L, Denver, Colorado 80204. I really like this website.
- **www.gsha.net** is the website for the Genealogical Society of Hispanic America. This very active society is dedicated to assisting those of Hispanic ancestry research their roots. A small membership fee allows members to access scores of resources to assist their research. The society offers access to publications produced by *El Escritorio* (The Writing Desk), which is a publishing and research company focusing on the Hispanic, Mexican American, Chicano and Native American Communities in Colorado, New Mexico and the Borderlands.
- Another excellent Internet resource is the AOL Hispanic Special Interest Group, which is accessed at **users.aol.com/mrosado007/index.htm** (note: no *www* is necessary). Located in AOL's Genealogy Forum (keyword: *roots*), the site promotes and discusses all aspects of Hispanic

genealogy. Its charter says they're not a formal society or club, and as such there is no membership fee. They serve as a very focused entry to other genealogical websites and resources.

• This is not the same as AOL's Genealogy Forum, **www.genealogyforum.com**, which is also helpful to those researching their Hispanic roots. From the home page, click on any of several topics, and you'll be taken to a link that may be of use to you. Click on the *Messages* icon and you'll be taken to a message board where individuals are posting information about various individuals. Perhaps you'll find one of your ancestors hiding there. Under the same icon, look for *Ethnic*

A FEW SPANISH WORDS TO EASE YOUR RESEARCH

If you go very far in searching for your Hispanic roots, you will run into Spanish sooner or later. Here are a few words common to genealogical research you'll want to understand:

archive	archivo
aunt	tía
baptism	bautizo, bautismo
birth	nacimiento, nacido
burial	entierro, sepultura
Catholic	Católica
census	censo
child	niño
christen	bautizo
church	iglesia
confirmation	confirmación
daughter	hija
father	padre
grandfather	abuelo
grandmother	abuela
husband	esposo
marriage	matrimonio
married	casado
month	mes
mother	madre
parents	padres
parish	parroquia
son	hijo
uncle	tío
wife	esposa, mujer
year	año

Resources, and click on *Hispanic Resources*, and you'll be whisked to a host of new websites specializing in Hispanic research.
• And don't forget Cyndi's List (**www.cyndislist.com/hispanic.htm***)*, which serves as a nice portal to many Hispanic genealogical sites.

An excellent book on Hispanic genealogy is *Finding Your Hispanic Roots* by George R. Ryskamp (Genealogical Publishing Company, Baltimore, Maryland).

Irish Research

Inasmuch as this is a genealogy book written by an American of Irish descent, I had to put in a section on Irish genealogical research! Here are some fairly interesting genealogical facts about Irish genealogy:

• In the 1990 US Census of the United States, over 30 million Americans considered themselves of Irish descent;
• Another 40 million indicated that at least one of their progenitors was Irish;
• 70% of the travelers to Ireland each year say they have at least one Irish ancestor.

Doing Irish genealogical research can be enlightening and exhilarating. It can also be extremely frustrating. Once you leave the United States, headed back to the "ould country," you need to understand what records are available, and how to access those records.

But first – and by now you should know what I am going to say – learn all you can from your parents, grandparents, aunts, uncles, etc. From this perspective, Irish research is no different from any other ethnic research. Collect information, stories, certificates, etc. Perhaps your family has a tradition that great uncle Paddy worked on the Titanic as a welder, or that your second great grandfather lost all his family in the potato famine. Stories like these can provide clues that will help you locate your family.

Knowing a little history about Irish migration might help you pinpoint when and where your Irish ancestors came from. Many individuals assume that their Irish ancestors all came to North America during the Great Potato Famine that struck Ireland between 1845 and 1847. And they may be right. During that black chapter of Irish history, of Ireland's eight million residents in 1845, one million died and another million emigrated – most to America, although many headed for other ports of call, including Scotland, Britain, France and Australia.

But while that was a significant migration, the Irish have been seeding the world's population for many hundreds of years. My own ancestor, Teague McQuillan, left Ireland for the wilds of America in 1619, coming to Jamestown a scant 12 years after that colony was founded.

Regardless of when your Irish ancestors left the Emerald Isle, your research gets more difficult once your family roots go back to her green shores for a number of reasons. First of all, you'll discover that generations of genealogical records were destroyed during the Civil War that erupted in Ireland in 1922, a sad and lamentable fact. It ranks right up there with the burning of the 1890 US census as one of the saddest genealogical events for genealogists.

Another reason for the scarcity of records was the fact that many simply weren't kept. Vital statistics that are a genealogist's best friend (birth, marriage, death records) weren't required by the Irish government until 1864. The Catholic Church, that great genealogical organization that kept records in all its parishes throughout the world for centuries, was forbidden by Ireland's conquerors (the British) from keeping records during most of the 18th century (although many did anyway!).

But don't despair...there is hope. The Church of Ireland kept records. Land deeds were kept of land transactions, wills were kept, and several censuses were taken. Passenger lists containing the names of thousands of Irish immigrants were kept. The Irish were very clannish, and often a clan lived in the same part of Ireland for many, many generations. There are several books that will be of immense assistance in finding where your ancestors called home.

The first is *Irish Family Names* (W. W. Norton & Company, Inc., New York, NY 1989) by Brian de Breffny. Another is *The Surnames of Ireland* (Irish Academic Press Limited, 1991, Blackrock, Co. Dublin) by Edward MacLysaght. Both provide excellent listings of many Irish family names and their counties of origin. Another outstanding book on Irish families and their ancestral counties is *The Complete Book of Irish Family Names* (Irish Genealogical Foundation, 1989) by Michael C. O'Laughlin. (Note: The first two books listed here are out of print, but some used ones are still offered through Amazon.com.)

Okay, let's say you have this craving to go to Ireland, the land of your forefathers (as many individuals of Irish descent do). You want to do some real roll-up-your-sleeves research yourself. Can you do it? Of course. But first, do all you can to narrow your search before you go to Ireland. And how do you narrow your search?

First of all, you need as much of the following information as you can get:

- Surname(s) of the individual(s) you are researching
- Names of parents, siblings, spouses (including maiden names of women), etc.
- County where they came from
- City or town they lived in
- Name of the parish they lived in
- Approximate years of critical events: birth, death, marriage, etc.

Even though you are armed with that information, don't go jump on an Aer Lingus flight and head for Ireland. Know what your options are before you go. Some options are:

• **National Library of Ireland**, Kildare Street, Dublin 2, Ireland. This is the national depository of many of Ireland's records on microfilm. It specializes in Catholic parish registers. The office is open to the public, and you can go here and pore over microfilmed records to your heart's content. Before you go, write to them to determine what records they have available for the parish or diocese where your family lived – include all the information you are looking for. Most of the parish records from around the country are contained here on microfilm.

• If you know the parish where your family lived, it is possible that their names are recorded in the **local parish records**. Try and locate an address and send a letter to the local clergyman, specifying the information you are seeking, and asking whether they have records that the public can peruse. Most do, some do not. Don't just show up at the priest's door with a grin on your face and a story of your search for your great aunt Bridget Murphy (note: there are many Bridgets and many Murphys in Ireland).

• Ireland's **National Archives** houses many microfilmed records from throughout Ireland, including Church of Ireland parish registries, gravestone inscriptions, census returns, probate records, deeds and a host of other records. The address is National Archives, Bishop Street, Dublin 8, Ireland.

• The **Public Record Office of Northern Ireland** has microfilms of church records of all denominations for all of Northern Ireland as well as several of the counties of the Republic. They also have many of the same secular records as the National Archives, including gravestone inscriptions, census records, old age pension claims, Tithe Applotment books, etc. Their address is Public Office of Northern Ireland, 66 Balmoral Avenue, Belfast BT9 6NY, Northern Ireland.

An alternative to doing your own research is contacting the **Irish Family History Foundation**. It is a network of genealogical research centers in the Republic of Ireland and in Northern Ireland which have computerized millions of Irish ancestral records. For a fee, they will do a search for your family in the records for their part of the country. Their main website is **www.irishroots.net** (catchy, don't you think?). There are Research Centers for each of the counties for Ireland and Northern Ireland, and they will search the most common records for information about your family. As of this writing, for a fee of about $70, an initial search will be made of available records for the area to determine if your family was from that area. If they were, and you wish it, for $230 (and up), the Research Center will do a comprehensive history of your family in that part of the country.

Before you go rushing off to Ireland to do your genealogy (it *is* a good excuse to go to Ireland though!), first check with your local Family History Center of the **LDS Church** to see what Irish records they may have. As of this writing, here is what was available to assist in your Irish research (unless otherwise noted, records are for both Ireland and Northern Ireland):

• Microfilmed indexes of births, marriages and deaths through 1958;
• Pre-1871 marriage and death certificates;
• Birth certificates from 1864 to March 1881 and from 1900 to 1913;
• Birth certificates for Ireland from 1930 through 1955;
• Birth, marriage and death certificates for Northern Ireland from 1922 through 1959.
• Deeds and tax records
• Census records
• Estate and probate records
• Family histories
• Occupational and school records
• Military service records

Along with other miscellaneous records and family histories, the Family History Library in Salt Lake City has more than 3,000 books, over 11,500 microfilms and 3,000 microfiche containing information about the people of Ireland. Virtually all of these records are available to you no matter where you live by making a visit to the Family History Center at the local LDS chapel nearest where to you live.

A publication entitled *Research Outline: Ireland* is available from the LDS Church Distribution Center for a nominal fee. It is an outstanding overview of research strategies, available records, and recommendations to make your Irish genealogical search a successful one. You may contact the Distribution Center by calling them at 800/537-5950.

AOL has a Genealogy Forum website *(**www.genealogyforum.com**)* that is helpful to those researching their Irish roots. From the home page, click on any of several topics, and you'll be taken to a link that may be of use to you. Click on the *Messages* icon and you'll be taken to a message board where individuals are posting information about various individuals. Perhaps you'll find one of your ancestors hiding there. Under the same icon, look for *Ethnic Resources*, and click on *Irish Resources*, and you'll be whisked to a host of new websites specializing in Irish research.

Other Ethnic-Specific Research

As much as I would like to address specific research techniques and help uncover sources of information for the countless other ethnic groups, it is simply beyond the scope of a volume this size. However, here are a few tips that may yield results for you:

From your Internet search engine, type the name of your ethnic group or the country from which the ancestor you are searching came, followed by the word genealogy (for example: Scandinavian genealogy, German genealogy, Chile genealogy, etc.). You'll be surprised at the number of websites you find that are dedicated to these areas of genealogy. And more often than not, many of those websites will have links to other websites that will also be focused on the area of the world or the ethnicity you are seeking.

Go to your local library and visit their genealogy section. They will likely have at least a few books on the areas of research you are seeking. If they do not have a particular book, inter-library loans can almost always be arranged so that you can get the books to review.

Find your local Family History Center. They will provide a gateway to the largest genealogy library in the world. You can go to the FamilySearch website (www.familysearch.org) to search for the Family History Center nearest to you.

Check out family history organizations, genealogy societies, etc. that have been formed to further research on a particular family name or for a particular country. You may find these on the Internet, in your local library, or in the phone book.

Learn the history of the peoples or countries you are researching. A knowledge of the history of a particular ethnic group or country will help you understand things that may assist your research. For example, if the family tradition is that your great uncle Paddy came to America as a ten year old when his family all died in the Great Potato Famine in Ireland, then you immediately know that he was probably born between 1835 and 1837. If you know the dates of the Great Potato Famine (1845 to 1847) you can easily calculate that he must have been born about ten years earlier. That is a good clue with which to begin – or further – your search.

Traveling to Unearth Your Roots

Even though records are available via the Internet and on microfilm and microfiche, if you are able to travel to the land of your ancestors' nativity, it is a wonderful experience that will likely live long in your memory. But before you go, here are a few suggestions that will make your trip a little more enjoyable, and hopefully, a little more fruitful from a genealogical standpoint:

• Do all you can to pinpoint what part of the country your relatives came from. Don't just show up in the country and hope to find where they lived. Find their town or county if at all possible.

- If at all possible, contact distant relatives living in the same part of the country where your relatives came from. Because of the research he had done, Alex Haley, the author of *Roots*, was able to locate the obscure African village where his ancestors came from, and he was able to visit there and establish a link with his past.
- Before you go, gather as many of your genealogical documents as you can that might be of assistance to you during your journey. Documents that list dates and places are particularly useful. Don't rely on your memory alone to guide you. Parish names, towns, counties, etc. are all clues that may help you locate the place of your ancestors' births and lives. (Note: make copies of these documents – you don't want to lose them in redirected luggage!)
- Determine beforehand how you will travel in the country you are visiting. Does rail service go to the area of the country you wish to travel to? How about bus service? Or would a rental car better serve your needs?
- Before going, try to locate where original records might be kept. Are they kept in the local parish church, or have the records been centralized to a national or county office or someplace else? Are they accessible, and if so, what hours are they available?

One of the most remarkable genealogical experiences I have had was when I traveled to the land of my forefathers – Ireland. Five of my eight great grandparents' surnames are Irish, so I have a special fondness for the Emerald Isle in my heart. Before my first trip there, I decided to try and contact some long-lost cousins. Never shy, I decided on a bold plan. First of all, it required a letter written to my Irish cousins. This is what I wrote:

Dear McQuillan Family,

Greetings from your long-lost American cousin! Doubtless you were unaware that you had a long-lost American cousin, at least not this one. But you do. In 1619 my tenth-great grandfather Teague McQuillan left County Antrim to see if he could improve his fortunes in the wilds of America. Ten generations later here I am, intensely interested in visiting the part of Ireland he left so long ago.

But that's not all. I am as interested in meeting other members of the McQuillan family as I am in seeing the Emerald Isle. Hence my letter. In May of next year, my wife and I are planning to visit Ireland and would like to be able to visit some of the cousins as well as the part of Ireland Teague was from. We will be in Northern Ireland from May 3 through May 10, and would love to stop by and meet you. Please let me know if you will be available during that time, and we'll arrange our schedule to meet with you.

I know this may seem rather presumptuous and just a bit bold, but

I really am interested in meeting other members of the McQuillan Clan, however distant along the family tree they may be. Thanks, and I look forward to meeting with you when we are there.
    – Daniel Quillen

After I wrote the letter, I made twenty copies. Then, from a map of Northern Ireland, I selected twenty small towns in County Antrim, where my ancestor was from. (I think something like this will work better with small towns rather than larger cities.) I addressed each envelope with the family name and the name of one of the towns. For example, one of the letters was addressed as follows: *McQuillan Family, Larne, Northern Ireland.*

And then, in the bottom left-hand corner of the front of the envelope I wrote: *POSTMASTER: PLEASE DELIVER THIS LETTER TO ANY McQUILLAN FAMILY IN THE VICINITY.*

I sent the letters six months prior to our trip to Ireland. I was delighted to receive seven responses to my rather unorthodox method of contacting family. But the results were marvelous! We met a number of these Irish families, were entertained in their homes, and they showed us great kindness. We left much richer for our time with them.

As a special bonus, they provided us with a wonderful genealogical treasure. Literally hundreds of names were provided to us, members of the family that I had not previously known about. They took us to the "old homestead," prowled through graveyards with us helping us locate the gravestones of past relatives, and a dozen other genealogical kindnesses. In fact, they introduced us to the "County Genealogist." He was a man whose father had prided himself in knowing all there was to know about all the principal families of the county, and who had passed the genealogical baton on to his son before his death. The son – the latest County Genealogist – was able to share stories about the family, and even provided copies of articles that had been written through the years about the medieval adventures of several of my ancestors.

So, if you are of Irish extraction, give it a try. I can vouch for its success in Ireland. If you are not Irish (how sad – but I suppose not everyone is so fortunate), try it with the land of your ancestors' nativity. What's the worst thing that could happen? The main risk, as I see it, is that the letters might be tossed in the garbage by postal workers who don't want to be bothered. But what if they are delivered? What if a distant relative responds? Cousin or not, you're sure to meet some wonderful people, and you'll likely establish some long-lasting friendships.

Ethnic Research Checklist

____ Identify an ancestor you would like to do research for.

___ Decide what you want to learn about him or her.

___ Write down everything you know about this ancestor – names, dates, locations, etc. Include information gleaned from family traditions.

___ Understand what ethnic research records are available to research.

___ Understand the process for accessing the various ethnic research sources (Internet, periodicals, genealogical societies, books, etc.).

___ If you are traveling to the land of your ancestors' nativity, make copies of all the genealogical information you have.

Additional Resources

Blankenship, Bob, *Cherokee Roots, Volume 1 & 2: Western Cherokee Rolls,* Cherokee Roots, 2nd edition (June 1992)

Burroughs, Tony, *Black Roots: A Beginners Guide to Tracing the African-American Family Tree,* Fireside Books, (February 2001)

de Breffny, Brian, *Irish Family Names,* W. W. Norton & Company, Inc., New York, NY (1989)

Gormley, Myra Vanderpool *Cherokee Connections,* Genealogical Publishing Company (January 2002)

Howell, Barbara Thompson, *How to Trace Your African-American Roots: Discovering Your Unique History,* Citadel Printing (January 1999)

MacLysaght, Edward, *The Surnames of Ireland,* Irish Academic Press Limited (1991)

McClure, Tony Mack, *Cherokee Proud,* Chu-Nan-Nee Books, 2nd edition (1998)

O'Laughlin, Michael C. *The Complete Book of Irish Family Names*, Irish Genealogical Foundation (1989)

Ryskamp, George R. Ryskamp, *Finding Your Hispanic Roots,* Genealogical Publishing Company.

Woodtor, Dee Parmer, *Finding a Place Called Home: A Guide to African-American Genealogy and Historical Identity,* Random House Publishing (1999)

Research Outline: Jewish Genealogy, Church of Jesus Christ of Latter-day Saints

14. Is Anyone Out There?

Undoubtedly, as you begin researching your family tree, you will run across other genealogists who are also interested in some of your ancestors. It may be an aunt you didn't know had an interest in genealogy, or it may be a distant cousin who happened to tie into your family through marriage. Regardless, sometimes these chance encounters can result in moving far beyond where you are on the family tree, or allowing that person to move far beyond where they currently are in their research on the family tree. Either way, it is a win-win situation for both individuals.

Don't pass on the opportunity to strike up a conversation with these fellow genealogists. They may have access to information you don't have. No matter how good you have gotten at ferreting out information from courthouses, census records, vital statistics, etc., these individuals may have things like old family Bibles, family papers like divorce papers, military discharges, marriage licenses, etc. And when you have information like this, there is an incredible sense of satisfaction in sharing it. Networking and sharing research are two of the hallmarks of successful genealogists.

Consider the following example that happened while I was researching this book. In an effort to provide meaningful examples to share with my readers, I was trying to pin down some additional information on my great grandfather. As detailed in the chapter on censuses, I began to think that he was born in Tennessee. The most likely location was Sullivan County, Tennessee, as that is where his father was born, and it was right across the state line from where my great grandfather grew up.

While searching the Internet for clues, I came across a website for the Sullivan County, Tennessee Genealogy Society. As I checked it out, I saw that they had a list of the surnames their members were working on, and my surname was among them. It also provided the name and e-mail address of the individual who was working on the Quillen line. I fired off an e-mail to him introducing myself. He responded almost immediately, and we determined that his 3rd great grandfather was my 4th great grandfather. He also indicated that he used **Personal Ancestral File (PAF) software**, and that if I had compatible software he would be happy to send me the genealogical records he had. I responded affirmatively, and within a day he sent me a large file containing all the individuals for whom he had done research – over 33,000 names, over 3,600 of whom had the surname Quillen!

So how do you contact individuals who are working on your line of the family? Sometimes when you run across them, you'll find only a name of the researcher with no address. Sometimes the address that you discover is many years and several expired forwarding address cards old. What then? Or – what if you want to see if there is anyone out there who is working on your line?

There are a number of avenues to pursue in searching for fellow genealogists. Following are a couple that I have had success with.

The Internet

Once again, this juggernaut of genealogical research comes to the aid of genealogists. Numerous websites provide an effective and relatively accurate means of identifying and contacting fellow genealogists, as well as contacting members of the family that might be able to provide information on an ancestor. These website are excellent electronic versions of the white pages of your local directory. Except they provide you access to the white pages in any locality in the nation. Several that I have used to locate others are **www.people.yahoo.com**, **www.switchboard.com**, and **www.whitepages.com**. The first two also allow you to search for e-mail addresses.

So how do these work, and how do you use them? While writing this book I was also doing some genealogical research on one of my family lines. I found that someone had been working on one of my lines. He had placed a query on a message board looking for information about members of my family. Unfortunately, he had placed this query on the message board a year ago, and the e-mail address he posted was no longer working. I noticed that the e-mail address looked like his initials and his last name. Armed with that little bit of information, I went to one of the above-mentioned websites. With just a few keystrokes, I found both his home and e-mail addresses as well as his home phone. To get this information, I just searched in the states surrounding the area where people generally are from who do research on my family. We were able to connect with one another and share information.

Message Boards

Message boards are websites where individuals place queries, specifying information or families they are searching for. For example, the following message was on a message board I visited recently:

> **Surnames**: Quillen, Burke
> **Classification**: Query
> **Subject**: Sarah Minerva Burke married to Jonathan Baldwin Quillen
>
> My great grandmother was Sarah Minerva Burke and she married Jonathan Baldwin QUILLEN. I think her her mother was Emeline??? and her father Thomas Burke. I don't even know their location for sure except they married in Lee Co. Virginia, and had children in TENN, and KY, possibly AL....love to hear from you.

The entry was followed by the submitter's name and e-mail address, as well as responses from a number of individuals who had information that helped this submitter with her query.

Magazine Queries

Just as you'll see queries about various families on message boards, genealogy magazines may also carry message sections where genealogists post questions about families they are researching. One of the most widely read genealogy magazines that posts queries is *Family History* magazine, published by Everton's Genealogical Helper (Everton's Family History Network, PO Box 368, Logan, Utah 84323-0368, Tel. 800/443-6325). Their query section is called Bureau of Missing Ancestors, and for a small fee you can post information about an ancestor for whom you are seeking information. You can subscribe to the magazine by writing to the above address, calling their toll-free number, or by visiting their website at **www.everton.com/shopper/**. At the time of this printing, the subscription price was under $30.00 for a 6-issue, one-year subscription.

Be a Detective!

Finding other family members or others working on your family line sometimes requires a great deal of creativity and curiosity. The more you have of these sleuth-like virtues, the more likely you are to be able to find someone who shares your interest in your family line. As you poke and prod in different and various places looking for your ancestors, keep on the look out for names of others who are looking also, or who are working on the same lines as you.

I have been known to go to the (electronic) white pages that covered an area within a 50-mile radius of the locality where my ancestors lived and found individuals of the same surname. A short letter or even a phone call announcing my search has often paid big dividends. A bit impatient by nature, I am always anxious to get information quickly. With long distance phone rates running 5 to 7 cents a minute with major long distance carriers, a long distance phone call is often less expensive than a letter to contact possible cousins via phone. As a bonus, you get information immediately, and sometimes you meet the nicest people that way.

Internet message boards, magazine query ads, the **FamilySearch website** and other websites often contain the e-mail addresses as well as postal addresses of those working on a given line. These are invaluable assists in helping you to find others who are working on your line.

Is Anyone Out There? Checklist

___ Decide who you want to do research on.

___ Evaluate the various resources available for contacting others who are doing research on your family. (Internet message boards, magazine queries, genealogical societies, etc.)

___ Decide which is best for your available resources – do you have Internet access? Cost of magazine subscriptions and magazine queries, etc.

___ Be persistent!

___ Be willing to share what you have for individuals who place queries about the surnames you are researching.

15. Professional Genealogists

If you think you have hit a stone wall, that you simply don't have the money, time or skills to go a step further on a given family line, are you done? Do you have any options at all? Of course. While genealogy may be a hobby to you, it provides a living to thousands of individuals and organizations around the world. And these professional genealogists will be happy to help you move your line forward – for a price. But before you rush right out and secure the services of a professional genealogist, there are a few things you should consider. Fortunately for you, I have included those things on the next few pages, so read on.

Is Now The Time?

I think you should ask yourself if now is the time to retain a professional genealogist. The detective work is the fun part for me, and the more elusive a given ancestor is, the more fun I have (okay – maybe I experience a *little* frustration!). Also, I have often found that if I cease looking so hard for someone and turn my attention to other family members – like the spouse, siblings, parents, etc., invariably I stumble across something about the elusive person that either solves the mystery for me, or takes me in a new direction where the mystery is eventually solved.

Do you remember taking those big tests periodically in school? You know the ones – the Iowa tests, or the California tests – the ones that were sponsored by the government? I remember my teachers and parents preparing me for the tests and telling me that if I hit a problem that I couldn't figure out, to leave it and complete the easier ones, then return to the ones that I was struggling with. Being an obedient child, I did that. Often, after just a few minutes away from the problem I would come back and see exactly how to do it.

So it has been time and again for me and elusive ancestors. I will often leave off researching for an individual when I hit a seeming dead end and focus on other individuals or even completely separate family lines. Returning after a period of time (often weeks or months later), I would see a clue that had escaped me prior to that. Following that new thread often yielded the results that had escaped me such a short time before.

Okay – It's Time

So let's assume that for whatever reason, you feel the time is right. Perhaps you really need to continue in your search for a given ancestor to prove your membership in a certain Native American tribe, or to link you to an ancestor who came to America on the Mayflower. Or perhaps the genealogy is being done as a present for someone. Where to start?

First of all, since you will be paying for this service, decide exactly what it is you are looking for. Before you even contact a professional genealogist, know who you want to find, and how far you want the research to progress. Do you want one line followed, or several? If you provide the researcher with a really wide array of things sort of related to what you really want, you may pay a lot of money, end up with a lot of information, and still not have found the individual you were seeking in the first place. So – be very specific.

Next, gather all the information you have already gleaned on the individual or family line you want researched. No sense paying a researcher to do the work you have already done. One caution here, though: make sure the information you give the researcher is all correct! If it is not, then the researcher is likely to waste a lot of time (and a lot of your money!) looking in the wrong state, or for the wrong parents, or in the wrong decade! Provide copies of any documentation you have that provides verification of the information you are providing the researcher. Also provide any dead-ends your research has run into, but make certain they really are dead ends. After you have done all that, it's time to decide on an individual researcher. Researchers advertise often in genealogy magazines, on the Internet and in the yellow pages. While you may choose any of them, I would suggest that your first stop ought to be to check with a professional genealogists' organization. There are several to choose from; here are the best:

The Board of Certification of Genealogists (BCG)

The BCG is a certification board with the following non-nonsense charter:

> *To foster public confidence in genealogy as a respected branch of history by promoting an attainable, uniform standard of competence and ethics among genealogical practitioners; and by publicly recognizing persons who meet that standard.*

Genealogists seeking certification will be expected to pass several gene-alogy-related tests and submit project work in the area they are seeking to be certified. The BCG offers five levels of certification:

- Certified Genealogical Records Specialist (CGRS)
- Certified Lineage Specialist (CLS)
- Certified Genealogist (CG)
- Certified Genealogical Lecturer (CGL)
- Certified Genealogical Instructor (CGI)

Each classification requires specific testing and/or project work to qualify for certification. BCG offers to serve as an arbitrator for one of their certified genealogists should a disagreement arise between the genealogist and a client.

A list of certified genealogists is provided on their website or from the address listed below:

The Board of Certification of Genealogists
PO Box 14291
Washington, DC 20044
E-mail: office@bcgcertification.org
Website: www.bcgcertification.org

The International Commission for the Accreditation of Professional Genealogists (ICAPGEN)

The ICAPGEN is an organization that certifies professional genealogists according to a set of oral and written exams. Applicants are tested in both theoretical research methodologies as well as in the location and use of original documents unique to their regional areas. Research strategies, knowledge of available documents and their contents are all part of the ICAPGEN certification process. In addition to being able to pass a test, successful candidates must demonstrate at least 1,000 hours of research in the area for which they are seeking certification.

Certification areas include the following:

- Eastern United States
- Midwestern United States
- New England
- Southern United States
- Canada (British)
- Canada (French)
- American Indian
- LDS Church Records

The ICAPGEN organization has over 100 certified professional genealogists listed on their website that you may contact, or you may write to the website below to get a list of certified genealogists.

International Commission for the Accreditation of
    Professional Genealogists
PO Box 1144
Salt Lake City, Utah 84110-1144
Tel. 888/463-6842
E-mail: information@icapgen.org
Website: www.icapgen.org

The Association of Professional Genealogists (APG)

The APG is also dedicated to furthering the ethical practice of professional genealogy. While the first two organizations listed above are certification boards, APG is an association for genealogists to join. Their website includes some common sense information about engaging a professional genealogist, including what you might expect to pay, payment arrangements, dispute resolution, etc. (Should a dispute arise between an APG-certified genealogist and a client, APG will serve as arbitrator for the two parties.) The APG website features a searchable database of certified genealogists. Just enter the specialty you are seeking (geographic, ethnic, etc.), and you'll receive a list of those genealogists certified in that area of genealogy.

The Association of Professional Genealogists (APG)
PO Box 745729
Arvada, Colorado 80006-5729
Tel. 303/422-9371
E-mail: admin@apgen.org
Website: www.apgen.org

Before you engage a professional genealogist, I'd recommend checking out several first. Find out if they have experience in the specific area you are interested in. If you are seeking help doing ethnic genealogy, find out how much experience each genealogist has in ethnic research in general, and their specific experience in the ethnic area you are interested in.

What Will It Cost?

Professional genealogists generally charge by the hour, and their rates are generally in the $25 to $75 per hour range. Some charge more, but they are generally specialists who work in highly specialized fields.

Financial arrangements are as varied as the people who enter into them. A popular and common way to engage a genealogist is to pay them a retainer to perform a certain amount of work. Once that work has been completed, then the client can decide whether he or she wants to continue with the genealogist's services. Consider setting a "not-to-exceed" price so that you have no nasty surprises.

Professional Genealogists Checklist

___ Decide whether you have gone as far your abilities and/or resources allow.

___ Decide what you can afford to pay a professional genealogist.

___ Go to any of the professional genealogical organizations to find a certified genealogist.

___ Locate a professional genealogist who has experience and skills in the area of the country or ethnicity that you want to have researched.

___ Share any information you have about the family you want to have researched with the genealogist. This will keep him or her from discovering research that you already have done.

___ Identify the specific information you want the genealogist to find.

___ Agree on a price (get it in writing!)

___ Consider a "not-to-exceed" price.

16. Help Your Descendants!

Consider the following scenario: You are helping your grandmother clean out the attic of her old Victorian home, and while working you discover a dusty old book in one corner of the attic. Taking it into the light, you open it and discover that it is a personal history that your 2nd great grandfather had written near the end of his life. As you scan its pages, you realize that he provided detailed information about his life and its joys and challenges as well as his hopes and dreams. Included on its old yellowed pages you find information about his parents, his sweetheart and each of his children. As a bonus, he wrote about various and sundry items that were happening on the national scene: a presidential election (and who he favored and why), how the family was weathering an economic downturn, his views on various wars or conflicts the country was involved in, etc.

What a find! What a joy that would be for you! Now - have you considered that you have it within your power to provide that very same information to your own descendants? If you wrote a personal history or perhaps even kept a daily (or weekly or monthly) journal, it could be your **genealogical gift** to your posterity. With a little bit of effort on your part, such a document could preserve important genealogical information for your children, grandchildren and beyond. It could provide a peek into your soul if you share your feelings and thoughts about the life around you.

Writing a Personal History

I have to make a confession: I started writing a personal history at least a half dozen times before I finally found a formula that worked and allowed me to finish it. But like so many other things that are worthwhile, sometimes persistence is the greatest asset you can have to accomplish something – but a formula helps too.

After trying several different methods, I finally hit on a pretty simple and successful one. Following are the steps I followed to successfully complete my personal history:

- Write down a list of "chapters" that you would like to have in your personal history.
- Under each chapter heading, write a list of experiences or information that should be included in that chapter.
- Decide on a time during the week that you will write on a *regular* basis.
- Decide whether you want to include photographs in your history.
- Begin writing.
- Continue writing.
- Just do it!

Chapters

Begin your personal history by writing down a list of chapter headings. This will be the beginning of your personal history. If you are like me, the number of chapters will grow as you think of experiences that do not fit into an existing chapter; when that happens, just start another chapter heading. Don't just write the chapters down in a Table of Contents, but write them on separate pages of a pad of paper or separate them by page breaks if you are using a computer.

Next, spend a few minutes with each chapter and write down a list of everything you think should go into that chapter. Don't worry about having an exhaustive list to begin with – I can tell you from experience that as you write your history, additional memories will come to you. When that happens, pause in your writing and go to whichever chapter the experience you just remembered belongs in, and jot down a few lines – just enough to remember what it was about so you can write about it later. Then return to the chapter you were writing in.

Below is a list of chapters that eventually ended up in my personal history. It is certainly not an exhaustive list, but the one that applied to my life:

- Summary
- Genealogy
- Birth
- The early years
- Schooling years
- College
- Friends
- Marriage
- Children
- Employment

- Memorable vacations
- Significant people in my life
- Significant personal events
- Significant world events
- Dan on Dan (my thoughts about me)

You will doubtless have other chapters that I do not have: military service, living abroad, my political career, My Life as a Spy, etc.

Now take each chapter and list events you want to be sure and include in your history, like this:

- Memorable vacations
    - Disneyland
    - Camping at Mt. Shavano
    - Yellowstone
    - Sand dunes
    -- The beach in San Diego
    - DisneyWorld
    - Western Europe
    -- Ireland
    - Scotland
    - Etc.

- Significant world events
    - Man walking on the moon
    - Kennedy assassination
    - Nixon resignation
    - The Challenger explosion
    - The Gulf War
    - Clinton impeachment
    - Bush/Gore photo-finish presidential election
    - Terrorist attacks on the World Trade Center
    - Etc.

Again, the reason for this list is just to provide a memory jogger for when you begin your own writing. Don't worry about making it an exhaustive list – just write down what comes to mind now. I guarantee you that more ideas will come as you begin writing.

Set a Regular Time

Once you have written down your chapters and have a list of events to write about under each chapter, it's time to set your writing schedule. Few individuals have the time or ability to sit down and write their personal history from beginning to end. Life happens to interrupt that plan for most of the people I know.

If possible, select a time that works best in your schedule. In my case, I decided to write every Sunday afternoon for a few hours. I decided to do it within an hour of returning from church services each Sunday. Some Sundays things came up and I was not able to write; but generally I was able to put in at least one or two hours each Sunday afternoon, occasionally more. Within a year, I had a completed personal history. Perhaps this time will work for you, or maybe it is an entirely different day of the week or time of the day. Regardless, the important thing is to set aside a day and time and then stick to it.

Additional Help

There are a goodly number of books on the market today that will guide you to look at your life and have a number of questions that will spark memories and help you begin writing your personal history. I have listed a few of the better ones at the end of this chapter in the *Additional Resources* section.

Keep a Journal

While writing a personal history is like writing the *Reader's Digest* version of your life, keeping a daily, weekly or monthly journal is more like writing the original text. I say a "daily, weekly or monthly journal" because it is my personal experience that with life's pace these days, it is very difficult to set aside time each day to keep a journal. But as with writing your personal history, I believe that if you set aside a set time each week, or perhaps each month (like the first Sunday of each month) to write in a journal, you will be more successful than if you try to write every day. If you also write entries for significant events – new jobs, the birth of your children, significant national events, etc. – then you will capture many important things that will be of interest to your children and others.

I have kept a journal for years, although I must admit, not as faithfully as I would like. But it has already borne wonderful fruit for our family. For example, when we celebrate each of our children's birthdays, they enjoy hearing my wife and I read what we wrote about them in our journals on the day of their birth. We wrote about what the day was like, the kind of birthing room, how long labor was, the doctor's name, and our feelings about each new child we welcomed into the world. (Even the teenagers like to hear these stories time and again.)

Each year on New Year's Day (or shortly therafter), I write a "State of the World" and "State of the Quillen Family" entry. It includes what is going on in the world and nation, who the president of the United States is (and my thoughts about him), and those kinds of things. Then I write about our family

Canada

CENTURY PLAZA HOTEL AND SPA, *1015 Burrard Street, Vancouver, BC, V6Z 1Y5. Tel. 604/684-2772, Fax 604/682-5790, Toll-free reservations 800/663-1818, Web: www.century-plaza.com. Several hotel/spa packages are available depending on the season. Accepts major credit cards. Twelve miles from Vancouver International Airport. Shuttle available.*

Located in the heart of downtown Vancouver, Century Plaza Hotel and the Absolute Spa at the Century are moments from most anything the city has to offer. Guests are just three blocks from Robson Street, with its superlative shopping and dining, and three blocks from the Vancouver Art Gallery; Pacific Center Shopping is five blocks away, and guests are less than two miles from Stanley Park and the Vancouver Aquarium. Once you've tired of shopping and sightseeing, however, Absolute Spa awaits at the hotel's lobby level, with a full menu of packages and treatments. It's one of four Absolute Spas in Vancouver.

Services: A variety of custom facials and moisturizing hand treatments; manicures and pedicures; massage including sports, aromatherapy, Swedish, deep tissue, maternity and tandem; Shiatsu and Reiki; a variety of body wraps and masks, including thalassotherapy and Moor mud; wide variety of hydrotherapy baths; waxing, electrolysis, makeup. Spa packages also available. Spa services include complimentary use of the ozonated pool and eucalyptus steam room.

Facilities: Ozonated pool and eucalyptus steam room.

Meal plans: Any spa treatment includes a light spa meal. Other hotel/spa packages vary.

Accommodations: 236 oversized suites with panoramic views of the Vancouver skyline, Grouse Mountain and the Pacific Ocean.

CLAYOQUOT WILDERNESS RESORT, *PO Box 130, Tofino, B.C., VOR 2Z0, Canada. Tel. 250/726-8235, Fax 250/726-8558, Toll-free reservations 888/333-5405, Web: www.wildretreat.com. Outpost rates begin at $469 per person per night, USD. Inclusive four-day spa packages at the floating lodge can be had for as little as $749 per person, USD; watch the Web site for specials. Combination packages, with two nights at Quait Bay and three nights at the Outpost, are $2,550 USD. USD rates vary according to current exchange. Accepts major credit cards. West Coast of Vancouver Island. From Vancouver: One hour via North Vancouver Air (800/228-6608); five hours via car and boat. Call resort for details.*

Two spectacular locations and styles of lodging are available here on the West Coast of Vancouver Island: Choose the 16-room floating lodge at Quait Bay or the Wilderness Outpost at Bedwell River, the latter being an ultra-luxurious enclave of safari-style, highly appointed tents. Quait Bay opened their new spa, Healing Grounds Spa and Wellness Center, in the spring of 2003; at the Outpost, among cedar boardwalks linking discretely placed guest tents, are spa tents—a rustic, yet opulent variation on the brick-and-mortar treatment room.

Both are set in one of the world's only remaining temperate rainforests. The Outpost's location at the mouth of the Bedwell River offers fresh and saltwater recreation among myriad land-based diversions in and around the stand of 1,000- year-old cedars.

Combining both land and sea adventure is the unique equestrian offering of the resort. On site is a retired U.S. Navy landing craft that ferries up to a dozen horses and guests to remote locations throughout the natural splendor of Clayoquot Sound, making hundreds of miles of trails and shoreline inventively accessible. A more memorable experience is hard to find.

Services: Both locations offer a variety of massage, including Shiatsu and hot rock, and body treatments including wraps and exfoliations. Quait Bay adds other treatments to the menu, including facials and paraffins.

Facilities: At Quait Bay's floating lodge, the spa hides wet and dry treatment rooms among cedar hot tubs and yoga terraces. There's also a fully equipped fitness room. At the Outpost are well-appointed treatment tents.

Meal plans: Inclusive. While the affable and talented executive chef, Timothy May, may encourage guests to ring him personally and discuss preferences and tastes before arriving, those who simply show up will not be disappointed. At the Outpost, guests might enjoy Clayoquot Sound oysters, Nanoose Farms organic wilted greens and Ucluelet goat cheese. A meal at the lodge may include free-run Cobble Hill breast of Muscovy Duck, oven-roasted and served with sweet potato shallot custard, and honey-braised Belgian endive with pan jus.

Accommodations: At the Outpost, guest quarters are 14' x 16' white canvas prospector-style tents, high walled and set on raised cedar platforms. Inside, handmade Adirondack furniture, king beds with down duvets, opulent rugs, propane- fired wood stoves and well-appointed bathroom, wash and shower facilities with hot running water. Outside, large porches with wood burning fire pits overlooking the river and sound. At the floating lodge, 16 rooms of similar—but walled—luxury offer brilliant views of the Sound.

DELTA LODGE AT KANANASKIS, *P.O. Box 249, Kananaskis Village, Alberta, TOL 2HO, Canada. Tel. 403/591-7711, Fax 403/591-7770, Toll-free reservations 888/778-5050 or 888-244-8666. Web: www.summitspaandfitness.com. Spa/hotel packages are available at a wide range of prices, from $299 up per couple, per night. Call the spa directly, 403/591-6227, for packages that are available through the spa only. Accepts major credit cards. Calgary International Airport approximately 69 miles from Delta Lodge; airport shuttle and limousine service available.*

Nestled in an exquisite valley surrounded by the Canadian Rockies at an elevation of 5,000 feet, Delta Lodge is approximately 60 miles west of Calgary and 50 miles east of Banff. Whatever the season, however, there's a wealth of outdoor activities, from world class golf (at two Robert Trent Jones-designed courses) and skiing to mountain biking, hiking, horseback riding and dog sledding. Hay rides, heli-tours, rafting and sleigh rides are also available. Yet Delta Lodge, host to the G8 Summit in June 2002, is just as impressive inside, with luxury as well as family-style accommodations, in two separate buildings; a variety of restaurants, and of course, the full-service Summit Spa and Fitness Centre.

Services: Massage including Swedish, aromatherapy, hot stone and therapeutic; body treatments including body polish, sea salt scrub, Reiki; wraps including Summit botanical, Alberta rose herbal, relaxing lavender, and marine algae mud; facials including aromatherapy, green clay, gentlemen's, algae refining and anti-aging; manicures and pedicures.

Facilities: Indoor/outdoor whirlpool; indoor saltwater pool; fully-equipped weight and cardio room; eight private spa treatment rooms; steam room and sauna.

Meal plans: Meal plans vary by package and a variety of plans are available. Contact the concierge or talk to a reservations agent to request a custom package to fit your needs.

Accommodations: Delta Lodge at Kananaskis is made up of two buildings situated 40 feet from one another and connected by an indoor walkway. The first building is the Lodge, with 255 guest rooms, including a variety of suites, family and loft rooms. The second building is the Signature Club, with 70 newly renovated guestrooms offering views of the Canadian Rockies. The Signature Club has private check-in and check-out, full concierge service and the private Signature Club Lounge, where complimentary continental breakfast and evening hors d'oeuvres are served daily.

ECHO VALLEY RANCH RESORT, *Box 16 Jesmond, Clinton, British Columbia V0K 1K0. Tel. 250/459-2386, Fax 250/459-0086, Toll-free reservations 800/253-8831, Web: www.evranch.com. The seven-night all-inclusive Baan Thai spa package, including accommodations, all meals and spa treatments, starts at $4,085 per week, per person; the seven-night, all-inclusive "Spa at Echo Valley Ranch Experience"* *starts at $2,111 per week, per person. Accepts Visa. Vancouver is 270 miles south. A variety of transfer options are available from Vancouver International Airport, including planes, trains, and automobiles. Call Echo Valley for details, and remember: The diverse landscape between the ranch and Vancouver is all part of the experience.*

If you've seen the movie "Legends of the Fall" and remember the ranch, then with just a little coaching you can easily imagine the surroundings here at Echo Valley. Swap out the stone construction for century-old logs, turn up the rise on the surrounding mountains, hang on to the horses and cattle, add a bush plane or two, some stout four-by-fours, and while you're at it, toss in spa facilities. A luxury wilderness resort offering an eclectic mix of adventure pursuits along with a full-service spa, Echo Valley tempers all the adrenal value of the British Columbian big sky with the pampering pleasures of any big-city hotel - minus the smog.

The addition of the Baan Thai Spa has added a unique "East meets West" theme to Echo Valley's spa services. The building is a combination of teak from Thailand (the interior), and Canadian cedar for the exterior. The top section is a complex of two Thai houses, a pavilion and an entrance gate, all surrounding a tiled courtyard. The Thai houses contain a spa treatment room and luxury suite. The Pavilion offers a shaded area to relax and drink Numcha, a traditional Thai herbal tea, while the landscaped courtyard is available for outdoor events.

The classic "Echo Valley Ranch Experience" is ideal for guests who want to enjoy all of the area's outdoor and soft adventure activities, including horseback riding lessons, guided horseback rides and hikes, all-day guided rides, 4x4 safaris to Fraser Canyon, and a gold-panning expedition. The Baan Thai Spa package includes spa treatments, accommodations in the Baan Thai suite; all meals prepared by Echo Valley's Cordon Bleu master chef; use of ranch facilities; yoga, T'ai Chi lessons and fitness center facilities.

Whatever you do with your day, be sure to have a hydromassage booked for the evening. A utopian treatment room makes this blissful therapy possible. In one place, your therapist will have at her disposal the use of a hydro tub, a jet shower, a steamer, and a wet massage table. It's 75 minutes of warm waters, herbs, minerals, and soothing massage.

Services: Body treatments including herbal wrap, skin care for the back, full exfoliations, and jetted showers treatment; massage including aromatherapy, Thai massage, reflexology, and hydromassage; three varieties of facial treatments; full salon services; an array of wilderness opportunities including horseback riding, hiking, white water rafting, hands-on ranch work, fly fishing, 4x4 touring, photography tours, and animal and bird watching.

Facilities: Treatment rooms including hydrotherapy tub, outdoor hot tub, sauna, steam rooms, indoor heated pool; fitness center with treadmill, rower, stepper, and circuit trainer; horses, float planes, fly rods, and more.

Meal plans: Three daily ranch-style meals as well as snacks are included. Ranch-style means hardy - included is fresh produce from the gardens, ranch-grown beef, pork, rabbit, turkey and chicken. A glass of wine or local spring water wets the palate.

Accommodations: Two lodges and three cabins accommodating a total of 20. A log lodge with six guest rooms, all having private baths. This lodge has its own sauna and outdoor hot tub. A separate lodge with nine large rooms, each with king beds, some with lofts. Seven of these rooms have balconies. Two cabins with private bathroom, sitting area, fireplace, loft and private deck. One log cabin with four poster bed, fireplace, sitting area, private deck with private hot tub.

THE FAIRMONT CHATEAU WHISTLER, *4599 Chateau Boulevard, Whistler, British Columbia VON 1B4, Canada. Tel. 604/938-2010, Fax 604/938-2099, Toll-free reservations 800/441-1414, Web: www.fairmont.com. Spa packages for two start at $629 Canadian per night. Accepts major credit cards. Whistler is 75 miles north of Vancouver, along Highway 99 – the 'Sea to Sky' Highway.*

In few places can you rub shoulders with snow boarders and golfers, wind surfers and rock climbers, fly fisherman and mountain bikers, snow shoers and hikers, all on the same day. In fewer places yet will you crawl over the snow boarders to make your way to such outstanding culinary experiences at the local Bearfoot Bistro. But here at The Fairmont Chateau Whistler in British Columbia, on a warm sunny day with plenty of snow still packed on the high peaks, you can experience all of that as well as some of the most expert administration of Ayurvedic therapy to be found in all of North America.

An erudite practitioner of the ancient tradition, Colleen Wight nurtures an impressive staff of diversified therapists, all held to the highest of standards. General massage therapists come to the facility with 2,600 hours of training, with specialists such as Shiatsu therapists adding 1,000 hours to that figure. Each has fine-tuned their skills with post-graduate courses and workshops. By the time they get their dexterous hands on you, they've had ample opportunity to refine all of the above training with countless hours of practical service.

While a variety of disciplines are practiced at Whistler, Ayurvedic traditions dominate the overall complexion of the spa menu. The body therapy called Swedana represents the 5,000-year-old approach to health and healing nicely. As your therapist makes the initial preparations for this treatment, you'll relax in the spa lobby, recording responses to a lengthy, sometimes probing questionnaire. Reflecting on your inner self, you'll notice natural light as it's refracted by the lead crystal windows, warming the rich hickory and pecan trim, and warming your soul.

Visiting with the therapist, you begin to understand the purpose of these questions. She'll have a word for your inner constitution: she'll call it your Dosha; in turn, she'll have a remedy for any imbalance that she may perceive in this Dosha of yours. Remedial measures begin with her selection of oils to be used during an initial phase of massage therapy, and then herbs for a later phase of steam therapy.

During the bodywork, an adjacent steam cabinet warms to the requisite temperature. In a drawer of the cabinet's lower interior, cheesecloth suspends the herbal prescription to all that may burden your Dosha. You may be reluctant to leave the massage table, but an herbal infusion awaits in the steam cabinet; with it, an ethereal time to detoxify.

Later, the handcrafted cedar cabinet is opened and the former table is ready for the third and final phase. Here, a skin brushing of chickpea flower exfoliates and cleanses. You begin to look back on all the questions, the oil, the herbs and steam, and you begin to appreciate the therapeutic value of such expert attention. In all, the experience has lasted 90 minutes. As the flower is washed away, one thing is clear: the folks up here at Whistler, they know their profession. And they know your Dosha.

Services: Ayurvedic body and facial treatments, including Swedana and Shirodhara; warm ginger and sugar exfoliations; body wraps including ginger and lemongrass; Vichy showers; esthetics, including aromatherapy facials, contour masks, and hydroxy acid exfoliations; salon services including hand care, foot care, waxing.

Facilities: 14 treatment rooms, including massage and Shiatsu therapy rooms; a wet room featuring Vichy showers; hand made Ayurvedic steam cabinets; indoor-outdoor heated pool; indoor-outdoor Jacuzzi tubs; eucalyptus steam rooms and sauna; fitness center.

Meal plans: Spa packages include breakfast.

Accommodations: 550 rooms and suites in a modern-day interpretation of the traditional chateau. Amenities include down-filled duvets, in-room coffee and tea, safes, data ports, hair dryers, bathrobes, and televisions. Fairmont Gold adds Jacuzzi tubs, fireplaces, as well as other amenities and services.

THE FAIRMONT EMPRESS, *721 Government Street, Victoria, BC V8W 1W5, Canada. Tel. 250/384-8111, Fax 250/389-2747, Toll-free reservations 800/257-7544. Web: www.fairmont.com. A variety of packages are available year-round; from $389 Canadian per room, per night, double occupancy, to $1,019, including breakfast. Victoria's International Airport is a 30-minute drive from downtown Victoria and approximately 17 miles from The Fairmont Empress.*

Steeped in tradition and rising regally on the banks of Victoria's Inner Harbour, the Fairmont Empress underwent a $45 million restoration in 1989 designed to restore the hotel to its original, turn-of-the-century elegance. All the guest rooms were renovated, yet a little bit of modernity crept in; a health club, spa and indoor swimming pool were added and only enhance the Fairmont's offerings. Willow Stream Spa has a huge number of imaginative treatments and packages available to guests. Of course, there's always afternoon tea in the hotel's magnificent tea lobby, surrounded by tapestries, moldings and polished, hardwood floors. For those with more outdoorsy tastes, check out whale watching, mountain biking, hiking, kayaking, or endless rounds of golf nearby.

Services: Massage including Swedish, aromatic, sports, Shiatsu, reflexology; facials, manicures, pedicures and waxing; body treatments including salt scrub and body polish; Thalassobath and a variety of herbal baths; traditional Kur treatments; a variety of day packages.

Facilities: Indoor heated swimming pool, indoor whirlpool, children's wading pool, two saunas, men's and women's changing rooms, fitness center with multi-gym, rowing machines, stair climber, stationery bikes and treadmills.

Meal plans: Meal plans vary by package and a variety of plans are available. Contact a reservations agent to request a package to fit your needs.

Accommodations: 476 guest rooms and suites are elegantly appointed, offering views of the city, courtyard, or a spectacular view of Victoria's Inner Harbour.

FAIRMONT BANFF SPRINGS, *405 Spray Avenue, Banff, Alberta, T1L 1J4, Canada. Tel. 403/762-2211, Fax 403/762-4447, Toll-free room reservations 800/257-7544, Toll-free spa reservations 800/404-1772, Web: www.fairmont.com. Highly inclusive spa packages for two begin at $561 per night. Accepts major credit cards. Eighty miles west of Calgary International Airport in Banff National Park; regularly scheduled shuttle vans from the airport to Banff Springs are available.*

Built in 1888 and styled after a Scottish baronial castle, the secluded Fairmont Banff Springs prides itself on a powerful grandeur that issues from its architecture and antiquity, as well as the surrounding wilderness. A striking Canadian Rocky backdrop combines with waves of coniferous forest to cradle the opulent refinements of the Fairmont. Outdoors, there's world-class golf, skiing and numerous other activities for taking full advantage of the surrounding wilderness. Inside are the well-done appointments of Willow Stream Spa.

Services: Body treatments including mud and herbal wraps, exfoliations and polishes; massage including sports, deep tissue, Swedish and Shiatsu; specialty baths including mineral, herbal and aromatic; facials including European, anti-aging and repair; thalasso and herbal Kur treatments; salon treatments including manicure and pedicure. Personal training; fitness assessments; weight-management counseling including body composition analysis and nutritional analysis; lifestyle management counseling. A full spectrum of fitness classes.

Facilities: A 35,000 square foot facility featuring numerous treatment rooms, men's and ladies locker areas, men's and ladies pretreatment lounges, coed pretreatment areas, men's and ladies whirlpools, saunas and steam rooms, three "waterfall treatments whirlpools," an indoor Hungarian mineral pool, an outdoor whirlpool and spa terraces. Also: an indoor, 32 meter saltwater pool and outdoor 20 meter pool; fitness center with a wide array of strength and aerobic conditioning equipment.

Meal plans: Some spa packages include breakfast, others include breakfast and lunch.

Accommodations: 770 well-appointed rooms and suites, some tucked in quiet corners of the castle, others taking in expansive mountain vistas. Consult a Fairmont reservations agent in selecting the room that's right for you, as an extensive variety of accommodations are available.

FAIRMONT LE CHATEAU MONTEBELLO, *392, rue Notre Dame, Montebello, Quebec, J0V 1L0, Canada. Tel. 819/423-6341, Fax 819/423-5511, Toll- free reservations 800/257-7544, Web: www.fairmont.com. One night bed-and-breakfast packages start at $197 USD per night; the Vie de Château Package adds a body wrap or scalp treatment, body exfoliation and massage for $155. Accepts major credit cards. One of three airports: Mirabel Airport, 55 miles; Dorval Airport, 80 miles; and Ottawa International Airport, 60 miles.*

After directing a hand-hewn flurry to craft and set 10,000 red cedar logs in the style and tradition of his antecedents, Swiss-American Harold Saddlemire had realized a dream. An aesthetic and logistical wonder of the time—having been completed in just four months—the 1930 construction of Le Château Montebello drew media attention from across the Americas. At first a private retreat for the elite membership of the Seigniory Club and then host to historic political meetings, guests have included Princess Grace of Monaco, Ronald Reagan, François Mitterand, Pierre Trudeau and Margaret Thatcher.

There's certain grandeur to validate such prestigious patronage. Take the three-story central atrium, dominated by its massive, hexagonal fireplace. Outside, there's the surrounding wilderness. The chateau offers a rustic refinement that, apart from the Swiss Alps, is hard to find. The effect on the soul is as soothing as any spa treatment on the menu.

Services: Balneotherapy, body wraps, exfoliations, facials, massage, and pressotherapy.

Facilities: 4 treatment rooms; health club including indoor 25-meter pool, strength and aerobic conditioning equipment including stair climbers, stationary bikes, treadmills, rowing machines, and free weights.

Meal plans: Some packages include meals; inquire with a reservations agent.

Accommodations: Within the Chateau, 211 guestrooms, including six suites, all with chalet-inspired decor.

THE FAIRMONT ROYAL YORK, *100 Front Street West, Toronto, M5J 1E3, Canada. Tel. 416/368-2511, Fax 416/368-9040, Toll-free reservations 800/441-1414, Web: www.fairmont.com. One-night spa packages for two, including specialty treatments, fine dining, wine tasting, and breakfast, from $699 Canadian. Accepts major credit cards. Lester B. Pearson International Airport or Toronto Island Airport. Consider VIA Rail: The Royal York is located directly across from Union Train Station and connected by an underground tunnel; luggage assistance is available to and from this station.*

A grand hotel with nearly 1,400 rooms, the Royal York is a Toronto landmark. In the spa, Elizabeth Milan, a leader in the Canadian spa industry, has hosted British royalty, Hollywood stars, and, with equal pampering and attention, the mere pedestrians of everyday society.

Connoisseurs will appreciate the Grapes of Bath package—at $700 Canadian, a true bargain, combining the best of Milan's hospitality with culinary decadence at EPIC, the Royal York's premier restaurant. The package opens at the spa, with a Merlot wine bath and a crushed Sauvignon body polish and wrap. The treatment offers a healthy cutaneous dose of the antioxidant vitamins C and E. A five-course meal and wine tasting follow, and then after a pleasurable night's sleep, it's breakfast for two at the Fairmont Gold Lounge.

Services: Massage, including aromatherapy, shiatsu, and reflexology; Ayurvedic Shirodhara; body treatments including Moor mud and seaweed wrap, salt glow and polish; facials including deep exfoliation and European; manicure and pedicure; electrolysis; full hair care.

Facility: Pretreatment lounge, 11 treatment rooms, pedicure rooms and full salon; whirlpool, saunas, steam rooms, full locker facilities; fitness center with a full range of strength and aerobic conditioning equipment and an indoor lap pool.

Meal plans: The $700 CDN Grapes of Bath package includes fine dining and breakfast.

Accommodations: Nearly 1,400 rooms and suites offer varied levels of luxury, with Fairmont Gold rooms being premier. In these rooms, guests enjoy such added comforts as pillow top mattresses and feather duvets, and such added service as evening turndown, pant press, and an exclusive concierge.

Mexico

LAS VENTANAS AL PARAÍSO, *KM 19.5 Carretera Transpeninsular, San Jose del Cabo, Baja California Sur 23400, Mexico. Tel. 52 624 144 0300, Fax 52 624 144 0301, Los Angeles sales office 310/824-7781, Web: www.lasventanas.com. A variety of spa packages including full breakfast and dinner, accommodations, airport transportation, numerous spa treatments, shopping excursion and full use of fitness and spa facilities are available; seven-day package runs from $6,800 to $21,500, depending on room and season. Las Ventanas al Paraíso, situated between San Jose Del Cabo and Cabo San Lucas in an area known as Cabo Real, is located 15 minutes southwest of San Jose Del Cabo International Airport.*

Located in Los Cabos at the tip of the Baja Peninsula, this luxurious resort and spa is nestled on fine white sands along the sparkling blue Sea of Cortez. Los Cabos combines a starkly beautiful desert landscape with one of the richest marine environments, encompassing both the Pacific Ocean and the Sea of Cortez. The latter is an underwater wonderland, teeming with sea life. The desert is a mosaic of color and texture with forests of saguaro cactus, sand dunes and stunning rock formations. All accommodations here are stunningly decorated suites, but once you venture out, there's plenty to enjoy as well, from sport fishing to snorkeling, diving, yachting, sea-kayaking, surfing, windsurfing and golf, as well as excursions into the desert and whale watching. Or simply enjoy a beach-side massage.

Las Ventanas offers guests a variety of dining options, including beach barbecues, dinner in the wine cellar, the Sea Grill at water's edge, The Restaurant, with food served on the patio or indoors; or the Tequila & Ceviche Bar.

Services: Body wraps and masks; facials; massage; hydrotherapy, balneotherapy and Thalassotherapy; manicure, pedicure and hair; body gommage and exfoliation; private or semi-private yoga, flex and stretch sessions; wilderness hikes; body composition analysis and fitness profile assessments; private training sessions.

Facility: Eight treatment rooms and 18 staff members make up the Las Ventanas spa. Treatment pavilion on the sand incorporates the therapeutic ambiance of the sea more intensely into the spa experience. The pavilion offers excellent ventilation and ocean views as well as complete privacy; guests can see out but people can't see in. At night, guests can enjoy seaside massages by torchlight.

Meal plans: Packages include breakfast and dinner.

Accommodations: Garden, golf course, and oceanview suites, with marble showers and Conchuela limestone floors, dual lines for modem/phone, fresh fruit daily, air conditioning, satellite television and music, terracotta wood-burning fireplace, in-room tequila welcome, CD players and VCRs; some suites feature private Jacuzzi, telescope for stargazing, and private infinity pool.

Caribbean

LAS CASITAS VILLAGE AND GOLDEN DOOR SPA, *1000 Avenida Conquistador, Fajardo, Puerto Rico 00738. Tel. 787/863-1000, Fax 787/863-6758, Toll-free reservations 800/996-3426, Web: www.wyndham.com. Four-night packages for two, including accommodations, access to Golden Door Spa and fitness facilities and one, 50-minute spa treatment per person begin at $2,655. Accepts major credit cards. East of San Juan and the El Yunque Rain Forest at Las Croabas. Transfer provided from Luis Muñoz Marin International Airport, San Juan.*

The only rain forest in the U.S. National Forest system, an exclusive golf club and the azure coalescence of the Atlantic and Caribbean all embrace Las Casitas Village, the first satellite location of the renowned destination spa of southern California called Golden Door. Inspired by the ancient Honjin inns of Japan, Golden Door spas aim to rejuvenate the weary. Here in the Caribbean, the weary are few but the formula works just the same. Combine it with the charm of 90 Spanish colonial casitas and the drama of the 300-foot seaside bluff upon which this place is perched, and there you have a true panacea.

With each reservation, tastes and preferences are noted. As you arrive among the polychrome pastels, white shutters and terra cotta roofs, you'll find a casita that's tailored to satisfy your every penchant. From favorite foods and drinks in the refrigerator to favorite reads next to the bed, guests don't miss a beat in making the transition from one home to another. It may have one bedroom, or it may have three; it will have a fully equipped kitchen, a living room of warm design, and balcony of exalting vistas. If anything's been overlooked, there's no cause to fret: each casita comes with personal butler service.

A 26,000 square-foot plantation-style structure holds the spa. Inside, three levels hold three moods. The Welcome Level conveys the sage presence of Golden Door staff. Here you'll absorb the Zen serenity of flowing waters and natural sunlight, as well as the advice and guidance that's offered to customize your Golden Door experience.

Step above to the Vitality Level, and you'll feel a kinetic impetus. In the movement studio, spinning and aerobics trade cadence with yoga and T'ai Chi; next door, you'll find steppers, treadmills and exercise bikes. At the wellness center, consultations and classes in fitness, nutrition, and health reinforce the surrounding spirit and energy.

The third level is called Tranquillity. Here you'll find something called Niwa, a Japanese reference to a place of rest. In the States, we'd call it a locker room; add Golden Door touches such as the therapeutic bath called O-furo, and the distinction becomes clear. From here, after a bath and steam, the therapist will escort you to one of 25 treatment rooms where you may receive a spirulina masque or pineapple polish.

Or perhaps it's a bindi balancing. As with any properly administered Ayurvedic treatment, the bindi balancing begins with a consultation to determine your constitution. With this complete, the therapist selects a combination of herbs and oils appropriate to your needs. The herbs are crushed and used in an exfoliating treatment that both detoxifies and cleanses and then, to further enhance the effect, they're used again in a wrap. Between the exfoliation and wrap, the oils are put to work in a light massage. In all, it's a highly individualized treatment – an appropriate choice here at Las Casitas Village.

Services: Massage, including classic oil, aromatherapy, parafango, maternity, reflexology, hydrotherapy, and hot stone; Ayurvedic including bindi, and shirodhara; body treatments including herbal wrap, pineapple polish, salt glow, mud wraps, aloe glazes, and spirulina; Kur treatments including thallasso and mineral; five facials, including a men's facial; fitness services including personal training, body composition, and fitness assessment.

Facilities: Movement studio for spinning, aerobics, stretching, yoga, and T'ai Chi; cardiovascular equipment including treadmills, stationary bikes, and steppers, each with its own television; Cybex strength training equipment; Japanese baths and steam; 25 treatment rooms.

Meal plans: Spa packages include daily breakfast.

Accommodations: One, two and three bedroom casitas with private butler service, fully equipped kitchen, dining and living room.

SANDALS ROYAL BAHAMIAN RESORT AND SPA, *P.O. Box 39-CB-13005, Cable Beach, Nassau, Bahamas. Tel. 242/327-6400-2, Fax 242/327-6961-2, Toll-free reservations 800/SANDALS, Web: www.sandals.com. All prices based on double occupancy, including accommodations, meals, taxes, tips, beverages and recreational equipment, start at $1,638 per person for seven nights for a deluxe room, and go up to $4,830 for a suite with concierge service, depending on time of year. Spa services are à la carte. Located on Nassau's Cable Beach, 15 minutes from Nassau International Airport.*

Voted the top Caribbean spa resort by readers of *Condé Nast Traveler*, and awarded the prestigious 5 Star Diamond Award by the American Academy of Hospitality Sciences for outstanding service, it would be impossible to run out of things to do at this romantic Sandals resort. Like the other Sandals' resorts, it's all-inclusive, meaning airport transfers, meals, taxes, tips, drinks and just about every other service are included in the price. And like several of the other Sandals' resorts, this one has an extensive spa, though services are à la carte.

Sure, you can simply lie on the white sand beach and occasionally dip into the turquoise sea; or if freshwater's your thing, you can hang out by one of the three large swimming pools and occasionally swim over to the bar. But if being active in the water is more to your liking, the resort has a variety of crafts, from canoes to Hobie Cats to kayaks to paddle boats. Feel like propelling yourself? Try scuba diving or snorkeling – all equipment included. If you need a break from the water, there's always tennis or volleyball; take a walk over to the Fitness Center for the more traditional stuff you can get back home, like weights and a variety of cardiovascular equipment.

Should you find yourself in need of more relaxation, there's always the Royal Spa. Located on the lower level of the Manor Building, the Spa offers a variety of massage services, reflexology, hydrotherapy, body wraps and skin and nail care, as well as facials and wax treatments. Check out the dry sauna baths and eucalyptus steam baths, as well as hot and cold plunge pools.

Should all this relaxation and beauty make you hungry – and it certainly will – there's a wide variety of restaurants to choose from, from casual to French, Italian and Asian, to an English pub offering traditional pub food.

Services: Aerobics and aquafit classes; snorkeling, kayaking, scuba, windsurfing, canoeing and other watersports; the spa offers a variety of massage, including Swedish and aromatherapy; herbal body wraps, facials, nail and skin treatments.

Facilities: Three freshwater swimming pools, three mini pools, six whirlpools; fitness center with Cybex weight equipment, bikes, stairclimbers, treadmills, elliptical cross-trainers and freeweights; two tennis courts; shuffleboard, volleyball; Jacuzzi; chess court; Spa with treatment rooms, dry sauna baths, eucalyptus steam baths, hot and cold plunge pools.

Meal plans: Meals are included with accommodations. Eight gourmet specialty restaurants serving a variety of cuisine, including French, Italian, Caribbean, Oriental and traditional Bahamian.

Accommodations: 405 rooms in 12 different categories, including deluxe, premium, luxury and grande luxe oceanfront. All rooms include air conditioning, king-size bed, private bath and shower; suite concierge service rooms include sitting area, mahogany four-poster bed, in-room bar, robes, free video library.

d a y   s p a s

Chapter 5

Arizona

RAPTURE DAY SPA, *3131 N. Swan Road, Tucson, AZ 85712. Tel. 520/318-3131, Fax 520/318-3232. Spa services over $60 guarantees reservation; 24 hour cancellation required. On Swan at Ft. Lowell. Open Tuesday through Saturday.*

Staff and clientele alike offer a very casual and comforting atmosphere at this Sonoran sanctuary that's owned and operated by three sisters. Walk into the first of the three buildings that comprise Rapture, and you'll feel a soothing hospitality that sets the mood for your morning or afternoon of spa treatments.

The first building is for warm reception; the second and third are each dedicated to spa and salon treatments. They cluster around a courtyard where you may relax before or after treatments, perhaps taking a Pacific Rim lunch, or meditating on the melodic song of a canyon wren. Or take your relaxation or lunch inside, where plush sofas beckon among towel-stuffed armoires.

The $245 "Ooh, Aah, ... I'm at the Spa" package combines a 90-minute massage, spa pedicure and custom facial. For the facial, Vivian is in high demand as her gentle demeanor and skilled service offer an exceptional experience.

The skin care center offers in partnership with a board-certified plastic surgeon pre- and post-operative service for cosmetic surgical patients. Medical skin care products, micordermabrasion and glycolic services combine to enhance the results of correspondent medical procedures.

Services: Four facials from $60 to $95; 75-minute microdermabrasion sessions at $75 or 6 sessions for $360; one hour massage from $60, 90 minute massage at $90; body treatments from $50 to $95, including a variety of exfoliations and wraps; manicure, pedicure and foot treatments from $20 to $55; waxing from $12 to $55; salon services form $22 and up. Yoga classes meet once weekly.

Facilities: Three buildings, each dedicated to an area of service: spa, salon and reception. Within the three, a courtyard for pre-treatment time and lunches.

SPA DU SOLEIL, *7040 East 3rd Avenue, Scottsdale, AZ 85251. Tel. 480/994-5400, Fax 480/994-0591, Web: www.spadusoleil.com. Accepts major credit cards. Gift certificates available. Credit card guarantees reservation; cancellations not made within 24 hours of scheduled appointment are charged at 100 percent. In Old Town Scottsdale, two-and-a-half blocks west of Scottsdale Road. Closed Sundays.*

Located amidst the art galleries in Old Town Scottsdale, Spa du Soleil offers a variety of treatments, including some delightful bath treatments they call "Taking the Waters." The most luxurious is the European curative bath, which includes a dry-brush body exfoliation, warm seawater-gel body wrap, revitalizing Thalasso spa treatment bath, body therapy treatment and an aromatherapy massage. There are shorter versions of these relaxing baths, as well as outdoor massage, facials, and more typical spa treatments. Check out the Chinese Tonic Bar, for an array of health-enhancing elixirs. Use of sauna and steam is complimentary with facial, massage or body treatment.

A variety of packages to choose from, including the two-hour Spa Treat, a full body salt glow, Vichy water treatment, hydrating body contour, European spa facial, followed by scalp and upper-body massage, $150. For those with less time, try the one-hour Terra Spa, which includes an almond-loofah body polish, nourishing botanical mud face and body masque, the Vichy water treatment and a hydrating body contour, $100. The five-and-a-half-hour Wellness Retreat begins with a purifying sea salt body polish, followed by Thalasso spa treatment bath and massage. After lunch, treatments resume with an oxygenating vitamin-c facial, a Remform therapy pack, and a reflexology pedicure, $365.

Services: Massage ranging from $40 to $65 for 30 minutes to $75 to $145 for 60 minutes; spa treatment baths, $50 to $95; baths with exfoliation and wraps, from $145; body glows and scrubs from $60; facials from $55; foot treatments from $38; hand treatments from $22; waxing from $8.

Facilities: Showers and lockers; 6 treatment rooms.

California

ANATOMY DAY SPA AND BOUTIQUE, *125 University Ave., San Diego, CA 92103. Tel. 619/296-6224, Fax 619/296-6236. Web: www.anatomydayspa.com. Accepts major credit cards. Gift certificates available in any denomination. A $20-per-treatment cancellation fee will be charged without a 24-hour cancellation notice; a cancellation fee of 100% will be charged for any missed appointments. On University in Hillcrest: Exit 163 at University. Open seven days.*

Sahar Slosser left a 15-year career on Wall Street when she purchased this property; her shrewd business acumen has combined with a highly affable demeanor to offer guests the very best in expertly administered services and treatments.

There's an exciting bustle in the surrounding commercial district of Hillcrest, but through the doors of Slosser's exemplary day spa lie certain sanctuary and solace. Choose a package and spend four or more hours in retirement. Hillcrest is dotted with great restaurants, and treatment packages that include lunch draw smartly on the local culinary talent.

Three packages include lunch: The $240 Eden includes a full-hour massage, essential oil body wrap, and customized facial with eye zone treatment; the $225 Vida includes a 90 minute massage with reflexology, customized facial with eye zone treatment and spa manicure; and the $185 Serenity includes a 90 minute massage, customized facial and spa manicure.

Look for the proliferation of the Anatomy example to continue with new hotel amenity spas that carry the name. As this edition goes to press, Slosser is planning a facility at the new W Hotel in downtown San Diego.

Services: Massage, including deep tissue, aromatherapy, pregnancy, reflexology, and stone therapy, from $75 for one hour to $110 for 90 minutes; facial treatments including moor mud, enzyme peel, glycolic hibiscus, paraffin, "C" and Sea (vitamin C and sea weed), and rosacea from $45 for 30 minutes to $70 for one hour and $90 for 90 minutes; a wide variety of facial enhancements including lip treatment, extractions, brow and lash tinting; foot massage and hand treatments and eye treatments from $10; waxing services from $12 to $65 and up; body treatments including sunless tanning and exfoliation; wraps including essential oil, seaweed, and thermal mud from $70 to $110; manicures from $20, pedicures from $40; cosmetic application from $30; five package combinations from $135; microdermabrasion, prices vary.

Facilities: A 4,000 square foot facility featuring two European-style facial rooms, two natural nail service rooms, three massage rooms, a body treatment room, two waiting areas, a dining area for day package guests, a consultation area and a retail boutique.

BURKE WILLIAMS, *1460 4th Street, Santa Monica, CA 90401. Tel. 310/587-3366. Web: www.burkewilliamsspa.com. Accepts major credit cards. Gift certificates available. Credit card guarantees reservation; cancellations must be made from four to eight hours prior to appointment time, depending on type/number of treatments scheduled. Between Santa Monica Boulevard and Broadway. Burke Williams has five locations in addition to Santa Monica: Pasadena, Sherman Oaks, West Hollywood, Mission Viejo and Orange. Call 866/239-6635 for reservations at any location.*

With six locations in the Southland area, you're never too far from a Burke Williams Spa. The 14,000-square-foot Santa Monica facility is the original location, opened a decade ago; Sherman Oaks is considered the glitziest. BW is known for their quality massage, though the signature treatments are imaginative, too. The most popular is the Hunter's Retreat, which starts with an exfoliating granular scrub, is followed by cleansing with wheat stalks soaked in essential oils, all while cascades of warm water immerse the client's body, which is then cleansed and bathed again. Afterward, light moisturizing oil is kneaded into the skin. BW also offers several types of herbal hydrobaths, an old-fashioned treatment with a modern twist. Following any treatment, clients are welcome to use the hot and cold whirlpools, quiet rooms, and steam and sauna rooms at no additional charge.

Packages are fun and imaginative but a bit pricey, especially with a 15 percent gratuity added to each. That issue aside, try the Day of Beauty, which at $420 includes a private herbal or marine whirlpool bath, massage, thermal seaweed wrap, spa manicure, facial, followed by shampoo and blow dry. The BW Bliss package, at $600, is all-encompassing: It starts with a private herbal or mineral bath, then moves on to pure relaxation massage, scalp treatment, then the signature Savannah's Surrender (mineral salts are rigorously massaged into your skin, then a warm, organic mud is applied. Cascading waters rinse you in preparation for a peppermint-menthol application). This is followed by a facial, manicure and pedicure, shampoo and blow dry, then lunch.

Services: Massage ranging from $85 to $105 for 50 minutes to $125 to $145 for 80 minutes; wraps from $55; spa baths, $35; facials from $65 to $190; dermabrasion, $210; hand and foot treatments from $75.

Facilities: Showers and lockers; number of treatment rooms depend on location.

SPA SEVEN, *2358 Pine Street, San Francisco, CA 94115. Tel. 415/ 775-6546, Fax 415/775-6078. Web: www.spaseven.com. Accepts major credit cards. Gift certificates available. Credit card guarantees reservation; cancellations within 24 hours of scheduled appointment are charged at 50 percent. Located in Pacific Heights, at Pine and Fillmore streets. The 22 Fillmore bus will drop you a half block from the spa.*

The owners of Spa Seven are an esthetician and massage therapist who've put an emphasis on a tranquil environment featuring holistic and healing treatments. Their Shiatsu treatment, called Golden Fish, involves rocking the client back and forth into the safety of his/her own body, with an optional half hour for Qi Gong. Also popular are abdominal massage for those recovering from surgery, and prenatal massage. Spa Seven is phasing out its yoga studio and instead is making that room into a relaxation area, with teas, books and comfortable seating. Clients can also relax on the second-floor, outdoor patio, which is surrounded by jasmine plants and has views of San Francisco's rooftops.

Spa Seven's most popular package is called La Vie En Rose, and starts with either an aromatherapy massage with essential rose oil or a body treatment using rose oil compresses and wrap; this is followed by a rose facial, then manicure and pedicure, $295 for four-and-a-half hours. Rescue Me for Mom to Be is a pregnancy massage using oils specially for the comfort of the pregnant woman, who is surrounded by body system cushions that adjust to any position. The massage is followed by a mini manicure and pedicure, and future moms leave with a gift of belly balm that works to release stretch marks, $260, for three-and-a-half hours.

Services: Massage ranging from $85 to $95 for 60 minutes to $125 to $140 for 90 minutes; eye-print masque, $55; breast/buttocks firming treatment, $65 to $120; cellulite spot treatment, $65; facials from $85; paraffin treatment and hand massage, $15; waxing from $15.

Facilities: Showers; 4 treatment rooms.

STELLAR SPA, *26 Tamalpais Drive, Corte Madera, CA 94925. Tel. 415/924-7300, Fax. 415/927-7528. Web: www.stellarspa.com. Accepts major credit cards. Gift certificates available. Credit card guarantees reservation; cancellations not made within 24 hours (individual) or 48 hours (package) of scheduled appointment are charged at 100 percent. Twenty minutes north of San Francisco. From Highway 101 North or South, take the Paradise/Tamalpais Drive exit. Drive west to 26 Tamalpais Drive. Parking is available in front of the building and across the street. Closed Mondays.*

Located just north of San Francisco and set among the hills of Marin County, Stellar Spa specializes in Ayurvedic spa treatments and products that focus on restoring and preserving one's essential dosha balance — your unique pattern of energy, comprised of physical, mental and emotional characteristics. Starting with a dosha analysis, spa therapists tailor massage or facial techniques with specific oils and herbs designed to address dosha imbalances. The Shiro Dhara treatment, for example, starts with chest, shoulder, neck and facial massage, and ends with a gentle stream of warm oil poured continuously over the forehead, the area known as the "third eye," to calm the nervous system and soothe the senses.

Be sure to try the self-heating seaweed mud therapy; the mud, filled with active marine minerals, gently warms and bubbles as it provides penetrating heat and detoxification. It's offered as an alternative to those who use heating pads or other chemical "heat" products for aches and pains.

The five-hour "Vacation" package includes facial, cucumber crush body scrub, Swedish massage and lunch, $455. Both the Hydration and the Nourishing package are $270; Hydration includes firming gel body mask, moisture fusion facial; the Nourishing package includes facial and remineralizing gel body mask.

Services: Swedish massage, $90 for 60 minutes, $115 for 90 minutes; deep tissue/sports, $105 for 75 minutes, $125 for 90 minutes; moor mud and remineralizing gel body mask, $100; body scrubs and masks, from $95; scalp treatments, $20.

Facilities: Showers and lockers; 11 treatment rooms.

TRILOGY SPA, *1301 Manhattan Avenue, Hermosa Beach, CA 90254. Tel. 310/318-3511, Fax 310/374-6452. Web: www.trilogyspa.com. Accepts major credit cards. Gift certificates available. Credit card guarantees reservation; cancellations or no-shows with less than 24 hours notice will be charged at full value. Downtown Hermosa Beach, two blocks from the ocean.*

Built to give clients the destination spa experience in a day spa setting, Trilogy specializes in original treatments using all-natural ingredients from Hawaii. The subtle, tropical feel permeates the spa but it's not over the top; colors are muted and relaxing. No matter what treatment clients come in for, all are welcome to try the complimentary mudbar, where you'll be able to sample from several body scrubs —

typically cucumber pear, lavender and peppermint — then rinse and relax under the huge waterfall shower. Need more time to relax? Take a seat on Trilogy's outdoor patio, which overlooks the nearby Pacific ocean.

The five-hour Trilogy Experience lets you choose from any one of Trilogy's Hawaiian-based signature treatments (including deluxe Asian body scrub, Hawaiian hot stone therapy or seaweed detox, among others), followed by full massage, facial, pedicure and manicure, $390. The three-hour Hawaiian Full Body Escape is just as tropical, and includes a macadamia nut mint scrub, Lomi-Lomi massage and pedicure, $260. For the same price, try the Kona Coast Journey, which includes a Trilogy scrub, wrap and massage, followed by a signature manicure and pedicure.

Services: Massage ranging from $55 for 25 minutes to $80 for 55 minutes; body scrubs, $55; body wraps, $85; facials from $50 to $125; foot treatments, from $45 to $85; brow and eyelash tints, $30; waxing from $15.

Facilities: Showers and lockers; 12 treatment rooms.

Colorado

TALLGRASS SPA, *997 Upper Bear Creek Road, Evergreen, CO 80439. Tel. 303/670-4444, Fax 303/670-7852. Web: www.tallgrassspa.com. Accepts major credit cards. Gift certificates available. Credit card guarantees reservation; cancellations with less than 24 hours notice charged at 100 percent of service. Tallgrass is located one hour from Denver. From I-70 West, take exit 252 to Evergreen Parkway (Highway 74). Go approximately 8 miles to Evergreen Lake, turn right on Upper Bear Creek Road, then go 5.5 miles.*

Tucked into the tiny mountain town of Evergreen, Colorado, Tallgrass Spa, which sits among gorgeous wildflower meadows, boasts stunning views of Mt. Evans and the Front Range of the Rocky Mountains. Give yourself time before the spa visit to enjoy the long, scenic drive up Upper Bear Creek Road, then have a cup of tea in the spa's wood beamed great room overlooking the Rockies. Lunch can be added on to any service for $17; be sure to call 24 hours in advance. Spa treatments for groups in Tallgrass's Sage Room are available with breakfast or lunch; there are four yoga classes offered each Tuesday.

The Tallgrass Full Day Escape starts with a facial, then offers a choice of body polish massage or herbal masque massage; that's followed by a spa manicure and pedicure, shampoo and style, makeup application, and lunch, $345. The Men's Tune-up includes facial, massage, shampoo, haircut and style, $185.

Services: Massage ranging from $85 for 50 minutes to $115 for 80 minutes; reflexology, $55 for 35 minutes; body polish, herbal body masque, salt glow scrubs, $70; facials from $55; waxing from $15.

Facilities: Showers and lockers; 7 treatment rooms.

Florida

EURO DAY SPA & SALON, *800 Formosa Avenue, Winter Park, FL 32789. Tel. 407/740-0444, Fax 407/740-0322. Web: www.euro-day-spa-salon-orlando.com. Accepts major credit cards. Gift certificates available. Credit card guarantees reservation; cancellations within 24 hours of scheduled appointment may be charged. Ten minutes north of downtown, between Fairbanks and Minnesota.*

Established in the mid-1980s, Euro Day Spa offers all the traditional treatments, from wraps and pedicures to waxing and facials, along with a full-service hair salon, but shies away from some of the newer therapies, such as La Stone. On the other hand, some interesting pain relief methods are available to add to any treatment, such as QGM therapy.

QGM infuses an area of pain or injury with very low frequency (7.83 - 13.5 Hz) chaotic sound waves, which are intended to break up the pain and open neural pathways to the brain for enhanced mind-body communication. This releases the body's vital resources for accelerated healing.

Create your own spa package from Euro's treatment menu or choose from the ready-made packages, like the Euro Delight. This package begins with an Rx facial (includes analysis, steaming and extractions, such as Vitamin C, collagen or elastin, depending on skin needs, followed by massage of the face, neck, décolleté and hands), followed by a black mud and aloe body treatment (sea salt exfoliation followed by warm black mud body mask). Finish with a reflexology treatment with aromatherapy or the spa's QGM therapy, a sort of electronic version of Qi Gong, $275. Water Body and Sole includes an aroma hydrobath with Dead Sea salts, one hour massage with QGM therapy or aromatherapy, and a choice of reflexology or pedicure with paraffin, $218.

Services: Massage ranging from $70 for 60 minutes to $90 for 90 minutes; salt glow, $60; wraps from $65; aromatherapy hydrobath, from $50; exfoliation, $55; facials from $80; manicures from $30; pedicures from $50; waxing from $12.

Facilities: Showers and lockers; 9 treatment rooms.

Georgia

NATURAL BODY SPA & SHOPPE, *1402 North Highlands Avenue, Atlanta, GA 30306. Tel. 404/872-1039, Fax. 404/817-7101. Web: www.naturalbody.com. Accepts major credit cards. Gift certificates available. Credit card guarantees reservation; cancellations without 24 hours notice are charged at 50 percent. Four locations in Atlanta; one in Decatur, GA; two in Chattanooga, TN; one in Wilmington, NC and one in Potomac, MD. Call 877/262-7727 for general information.*

Natural Body spas have grown from the single, original North Highlands Avenue location in Atlanta – back then a two-room spa, opened 13 years ago – to the now incredibly successful nine locations throughout the south. The services and products are top-notch but the service is pure southern hospitality and perhaps a bit different from most spas: down-to-earth without an attitude. Each NB spa has a retail area that sells all the products used in treatments; custom blends of oils, salts, lotions and body washes are available. While each NB spa has a similar color scheme and product line, they aren't cookie cutter copies, and every location has a slightly different feel.

NB's deluxe half-day package, at $320, includes massage, body treatment (anti-aging, detoxifying & exfoliating treatment with warm essential oil compresses, Jurlique antioxidant gel, followed by mud mask and wrap); facial, hand/foot treatment or manicure/pedicure. Includes spa lunch. The two-and-a-half hour Body De-tox, at $195, includes polish or salt glow treatment, massage, and seaweed or mud wrap.

Services: Massage ranging from $40 for 30 minutes to $100 for 90 minutes; heated stone therapy massage, $95 for 60 minutes, $135 for 90 minutes; seaweed body wrap, $100; salt glow, $50; hand treatment, $20, foot treatment, $50, add paraffin to either, $15.

Note: Prices may vary per location. Not all treatments are available at all locations.

Facilities: Showers; 6-12 treatment rooms, depending on location.

VISIONARIESPA, *1412 West Peachtree Street, Atlanta, GA 30309. Tel. 404/733-6400, Fax. 404/733-6868. Web: www.VisionarieSpa.com. Accepts major credit cards. Gift certificates available. Credit card guarantees reservation; cancellations with less than 48 hours notice of scheduled appointment are charged at 50 percent. VisionarieSpa is located in Midtown on the corner of 18th and West Peachtree streets, one block west of Peachtree Street next door to the Atlanta Ballet. By rail, get off at Art Center Station, exit on the West Peachtree Street side, and walk approximately four blocks north to the spa. Closed Sunday and Monday.*

The décor in this beautiful, four-level spa in the artsy Midtown section of Atlanta is Asian-inspired, with Bonsai gardens, waterfalls, koi fish and shoshi doors throughout. Located in a renovated house, a series of three lush, outdoor decks are available for relaxing and food. The fourth-floor deck has a barbecue pit and outdoor furniture and the spa is available for private spa party rentals. Besides the traditional spa treatments, VisionarieSpa offers wellness related classes and seminars including yoga, nutritional/fitness counseling, stress and anger management, life enhancement coaching, art therapy and T'ai Chi classes.

The half-day spa sampler includes a manicure, pedicure, Swedish full body massage, and sauna or steam, $170. A day at the spa includes a sea salt manicure and pedicure, paraffin wax treatments, customized facial, body polish, La Stone massage, sauna or steam therapy, and a shampoo/style, as well as lunch, $425.

Services: Massage (Swedish, shiatsu, deep tissue or pregnancy) range from $50 for 30 minutes to $80 for 60 minutes; salt glow, hydro pack wrap, herbal linen wrap, $70; moor mud and seaweed body wrap, $125; facials from $75; waxing from $15.

Facilities: Showers and lockers; 5 treatment rooms.